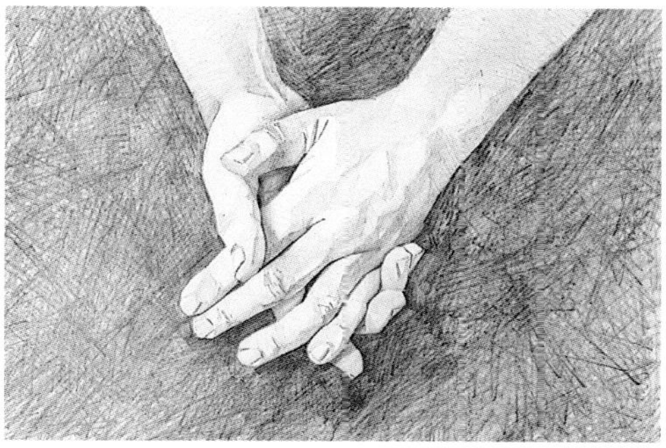

# D R A W I N G

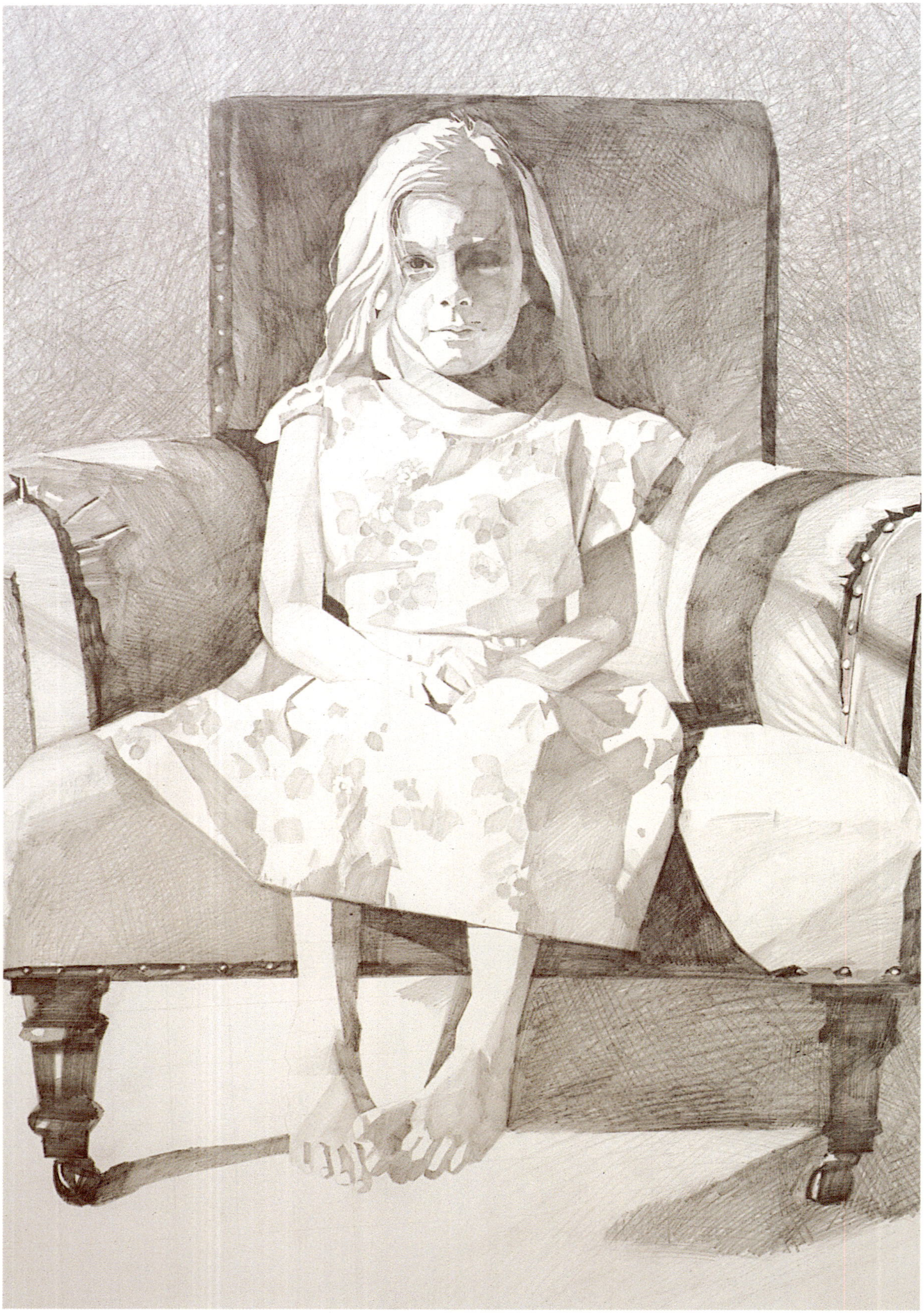

SUNBURST ART SERIES

# DRAWING

Ian Sidaway

SUNBURST BOOKS

This edition first published in 1996 by
Sunburst Books,
Deacon House,
65 Old Church Street,
London SW3 5BS



ISBN 1 85778 215 1

Printed and bound in China

# CONTENTS

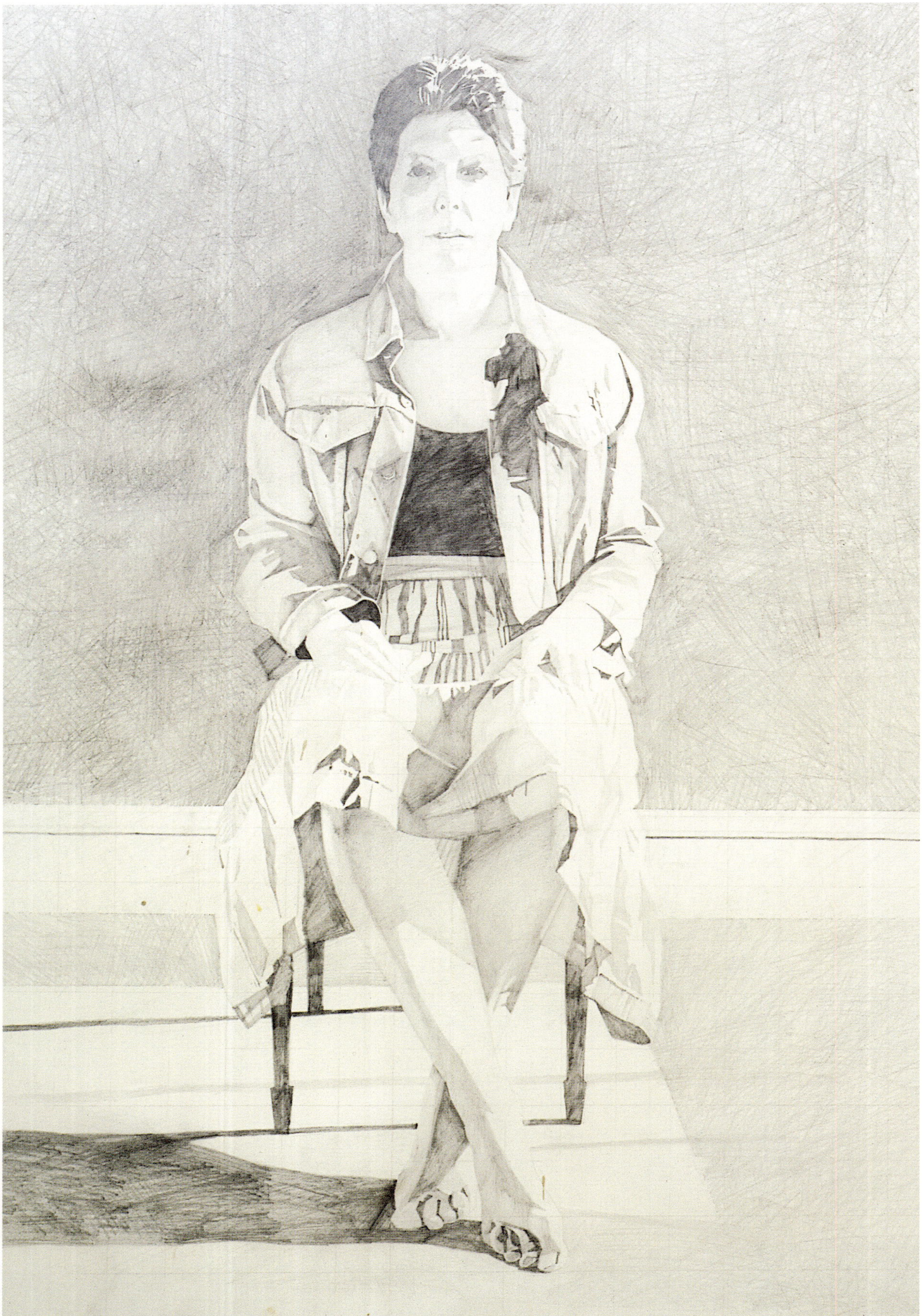

# INTRODUCTION

DRAWING IS AN intuitive and instinctive activity. However, to do it well it does require focus and thought. Drawing skills are acquired, and subsequently developed, by practise and repetition, in much the same way as the art of writing. Even in the age of the silicone chip, most of us still practise the art of writing daily, be it only in scribbling a shopping list or simple route directions for someone to follow. The opposite is true of drawing: it is an activity that, because of lack of practice, most of us forget how to do once we have left childhood behind.

All children draw – it is their natural inclination to reach for the pot of wax crayons and cheap paper we all diligently supply for them, long before they can talk – and as a race, humans have always drawn, as the prehistoric rock paintings found throughout the world so graphically show. Some of these drawings were made some 25,000 years ago, yet they are surprisingly sophisticated and pure representations. The people who created these remarkable paintings were not trained in any way to be artists: the concept of the artist did not exist. Instinctively, they simply drew and interpreted what they saw, and it is in this spirit that we still begin as children to express ourselves by drawing.

Young children produce drawings and artworks intuitively, for their own sake, completely without inhibition and early on in their development, without any sense or feeling of failure. With age comes an increased awareness and knowledge of how things really look, and in the search for exactitude we try to imitate correctly what we see, using increasingly difficult techniques. It is at this point, usually around the awkward years of early adolescence, that, embarrassed and frustrated with failure, we cease to draw, believing that we cannot.

Yet in spite of this the basic desire to draw stays with us; few of us can resist scribbling and doodling in the margins of telephone directories or on the backs of envelopes, and we do so almost without thinking. To fulfil the desire to draw we need to learn again and develop those forgotten skills, and, like learning anything, this requires time, effort and practice. It is by drawing that we learn to draw.

Forget failure: professional artists fail only too often, believe me. The work we admire, so immaculately framed and bathed in ideal light on the gallery wall, is more than likely the result of several less successful attempts consigned to the plan-chest drawer. To the artist, these unseen drawings or paintings are of no less importance than the work on show: they are a necessary and crucial part of the artist's creative development.

### 'Begin with the bones...'

Making pictures is a subjective process; while there are certain principles that we need to acknowledge, these are open to wide and varied interpretation. Indeed many of the best works stretch these principles to the limit. Leon Battista Alberti, a 15th century aesthetic and scholar, said: 'Begin with the bones then add the muscle.' He was referring to the correct way of representing the human figure; however, the laying of a strong foundation is central to all art, and the ability to draw well lays that foundation. The process is two fold: first, we need to relearn the way we look at things; and second, we need to learn about technique – the marks that it is possible to make with our chosen materials, and how to go about making them.

### How to use this book

This book deals with a range of drawing materials and media and the drawing techniques that can be used with them. Following the introductory sections dealing with equipment and materials, there is a section that shows the techniques that are used throughout the book. It is my belief that practising and becoming familiar with the techniques in isolation, without concentrating on making a picture, can help give confidence in handling the materials. The projects, which are relatively straightforward to begin with, gain in complexity. They combine a range of basic techniques with specific picture-making principles. You will be shown different ways of looking at your chosen subject; how to compose the picture; how to deal with perspective and proportions; and how to use light, shade, and line to create the illusion of mass, shape and form. But, as the saying goes, there are several ways to skin a cat – and for each project drawing you will also be shown several alternative ways of approaching and handling the subject matter.

It would be foolish to suppose that drawing is not difficult. There are no shortcuts or easy answers, but learn the principles and techniques, become familiar with the materials, and, above all, practise, for each time you put pencil to paper the task will become just that bit easier, and the satisfaction just that little bit greater.

# MATERIALS AND EQUIPMENT

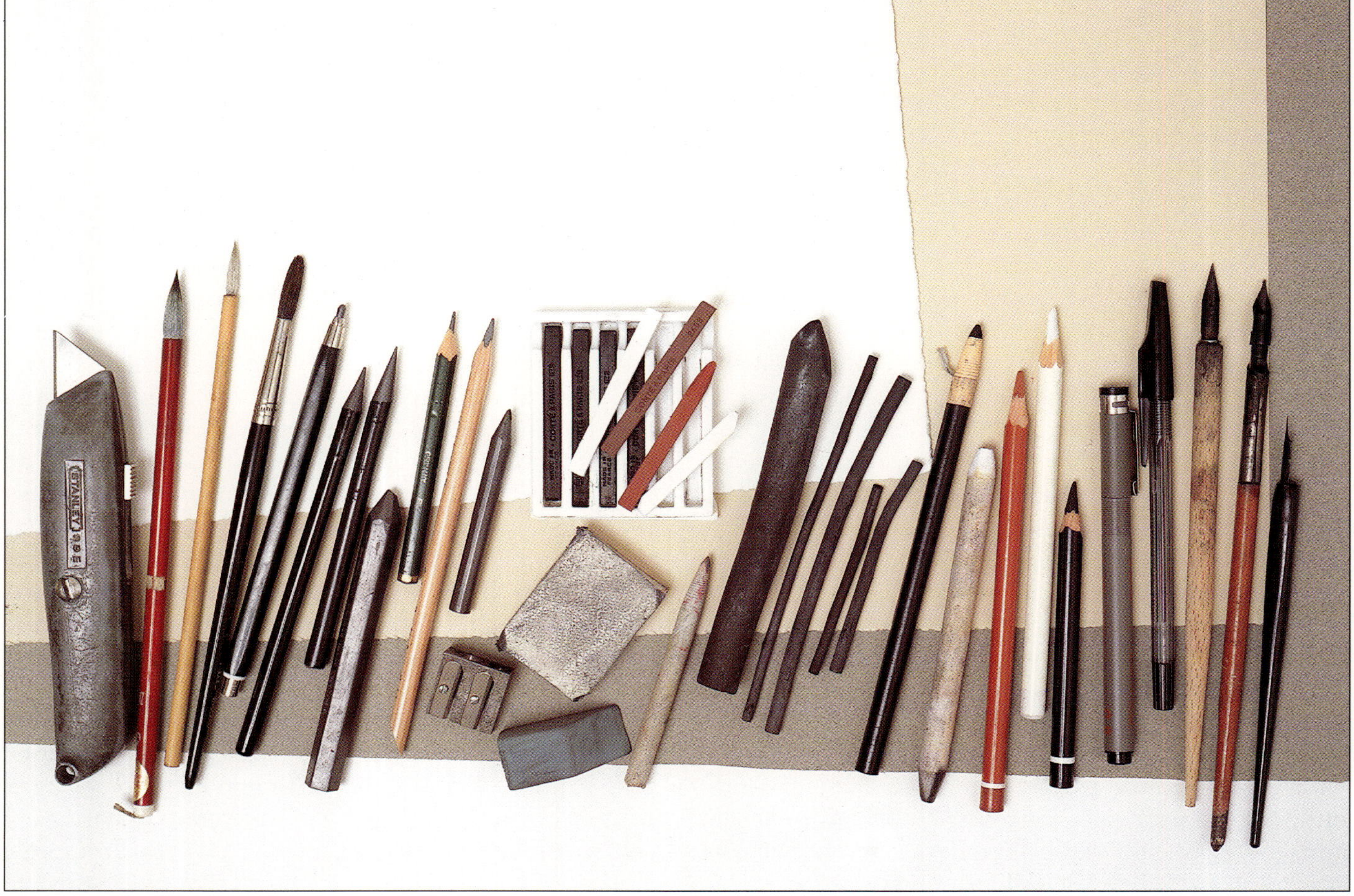


THE QUALITY AND SURFACE of the support you choose to work on are of primary importance, and can make the difference between success and failure. Therefore, the first material you should consider purchasing is the support for your work.

**Drawing papers and boards**

Given the bewildering range of paper and boards available it is little wonder that beginners find it difficult to decide which papers to use. Papers can be expensive, and making the wrong decision not only leaves a hole in the wallet, it can also make the drawing process more difficult than necessary. Common sense should match the paper with the medium. Charcoal tends to work best on a surface that has some texture, while it is preferable to do a drawing with pen and ink on a smoother paper. By experimenting with a variety of papers you will discover the ones that are best suited to your way of working, subject and chosen medium.

Papers and boards come in a wide range of sizes, textures and weights, and most papers used by artists are finished with glue, or 'sized', to give an acceptable and receptive surface on which to work. In addition, papers are either handmade or machine made. The handmade papers tend to be more expensive and are sized on one side only, this being the correct side on which to work. They are usually watermarked or embossed with the manufacturer's name, and have a ragged, or 'deckle', edge. Machine-made papers come with three types of surface: Hot Pressed paper, which is smooth, with little or no surface texture; Not or CP (cold pressed) paper, which is not hot pressed and has a definite tooth or texture; and Rough, which has a very pronounced texture. All three surfaces can be used, but Not and Hot Pressed present the best surface for drawing.

A paper's thickness is indicated by its weight: the heavier the weight the thicker the paper. Two systems exist for measuring weight: the first is in pounds and refers to the weight of a ream (500 sheets) of that particular paper, for example, 140lb, 260lb; the second is in grams, and refers to the grams per square meter of a single sheet, for example, 300gsm, 356gsm.

Thick papers can withstand vigorous, heavy over-working and multiple erasures when using a dry medium; when using a wet medium they stay flat and resist cockling, so they do not need stretching. For most drawing you will find that a medium-weight 90lb or 140lb cartridge paper is more than adequate. White or off-white papers are traditionally used for drawing, but coloured papers offer some exciting possibilities. There is a large range of coloured papers available; most are used for pastel, chalk or charcoal work and usually carry a fine to medium tooth. Boards are available with Not and Fine surfaces, and are ideal when drawing with fine technical pens.

Sketchbooks come in a multitude of shapes and sizes containing a wide variety of paper weights, surface types and colour. Choose your sketchbooks with as much care as you would paper, giving thought to what you want to draw and the materials you intend to use. Over time you should amass quite a few, for it is within the pages of the sketch book that you can not only practise drawing, but also experiment with marks and effects, so building up a reference of possibilities.

### Pencil and graphite

The pencil is arguably the most widely used and versatile of all drawing implements. It is possible to achieve a vast range of marks – from light, delicate, almost imperceptible lines to broad, dark, strong areas of heavily scribbled tone and textural effects – with just one, carefully chosen pencil. There are 20 grades of pencil: they range from 9H, the hardest, to H, F, HB, and B in the middle; then they get progressively softer, to 9B. The harder grades make lighter and finer lines. They can be sharpened to a fine point, which makes them more suitable for precise technical drawing where a consistent line thickness is important. For freehand work it is better to choose a softer grade: as the point becomes worn and blunt – which with the very soft grades happens surprisingly fast – it is possible to vary the quality of the line, giving interest and expression to the drawing.

In reality, rarely is one pencil used when making a drawing: more often, two or three of varying degrees of hardness are used. The HB pencil is generally thought of as being the ideal all-round drawing pencil, with greatest flexibility, capable of rendering a broad range of tone and line. I prefer the F; the line quality tends to be crisper but the tonal range that can be achieved is just as wide.

The pencil shaft tends to be either hexagonal or round. Hexagonal shafts give a firmer grip while round shafts enable the pencil to be rolled easily in the finger, making it possible to present a different profile of the graphite strip to the paper, without having to pause in your work.

Studio or sketching pencils are rectangular and flat, like carpenters' pencils, and come in soft, medium and hard grades. When used with the graphite strip flat, they are ideal for quickly blocking in large areas of tone, but when turned on their side they give a line varying in thickness. They may feel a little unwieldy and awkward at first, but with experimentation are capable of producing a wide range of marks, and are good when working large.

I find graphite sticks the most useful and easy to use of all the drawing instruments. They come in grades of softness from HB to 9B, and in a variety of thicknesses. They are the perfect tool for making marks. These solid sticks of graphite are either coated on the outside to keep the hand clean or, as in the case of the thicker hexagonal sticks, uncoated. Given the large area of exposed graphite it is possible to make the transition from fine lines to broad, dense areas of tone in one stroke. Care should be taken with the thinner, soft pencils, as they can break easily if held high up the shaft and pressed hard, or if dropped onto a hard floor.

Graphite can be obtained in the form of powder; when rubbed onto the paper with a rag or a finger it will produce a beautiful area of tone that can be worked on with a pencil or graphite stick, and lightened by drawing into it with an eraser.

### Charcoal, conté and chalk

The best charcoal is charred wood from the willow, the beech and the vine. This is the oldest-known drawing material, made in much the same way for centuries. Charcoal is a very expressive and direct medium; the boldness and clarity of the marks encourage the artist to work larger than one might with pencil. This can be very helpful when learning to draw, as it forces the artist to look at the subject as a whole rather than concentrate on detail. Charcoal is available in varying degrees of hardness and thickness. The thinner sticks are bought by the box but the thicker sticks, often referred to as scene-painters' charcoal, are sold individually. The thin sticks are best used for line work and can be sharpened to a point with fine sandpaper. The thicker sticks, while also suitable for line work, are used to block in large areas of tone, either by using the end or by turning the stick onto its side. Thicker sticks are best sharpened with a craft knife. Drawing with charcoal can be a messy business. If this becomes a problem, it can be minimised by wrapping silver foil around the stick, which will keep the fingers clean, by using a clean sheet of paper to rest the drawing hand on to prevent rubbing the drawn surface, and by periodically fixing the drawing (see page 12). Marks made with charcoal can easily be removed before fixing by flicking over the surface with a clean rag or using a large soft brush. A ghost of a mark will remain which can be removed with a putty eraser or left to serve as a guide for any redrawing. The marks left when redrawing in this way are known as *pentimenti*. Blending can be done with the fingers, cotton wool buds, rag, brush or tissues. However the ideal tool is the torchon, or paper blender, a tightly rolled paper stump – usually pointed at both ends – which enables the artist to blend and push the charcoal dust around the drawing.

Compressed charcoal sticks are made from charcoal powder and a binder. They are harder than traditional charcoal, making the marks harder to erase and blending more difficult, but they are cleaner to use. Compressed charcoal can also be bought as pencils encased in paper or wood. They vary in degrees of softness so are suited to finer work. Their one disadvantage is that, unlike pure charcoal, they cannot be used on their side.

Conté sticks, or pastels, are harder than charcoal and come in a range of colours, tones and hardness. Traditionally, black, red (known as sanguine), dark brown (or bistre) and white were used for drawing, often together, to produce beautiful works of great depth and intensity. The conté stick is best used on tinted paper with a slight tooth to provide a mid tone and a key for the chalk. It can be used to build up subtle areas of tone and shading by using the end (which can be sharpened with a knife) for hatching and line work, or by blocking in areas of tone using the stick on its side.

Like charcoal, conté sticks can be blended, but unlike charcoal are not as easy to erase. It is advisable to give the drawings a coat of fixative when they are finished.

All the colours are available as pencils, with the same advantages and disadvantages found with the charcoal pencils. Treat charcoal and pastel pencils gently; if dropped the strip can crack inside the wood, making it impossible to sharpen them without pieces breaking off.

### Pen and ink

Pen and ink has been a favoured drawing medium of the artist for centuries. The pen, or quill, as the word pen originally meant, has been an instrument for writing since early Christian times. The quill pen is made by shaping the end of a suitable feather with a pen knife and is capable of making the most beautiful of lines. A variety of feathers can be used, but it is said that the point fashioned from a crow's quill is the best for drawing. With time the point wears down and becomes soft, so it needs to be reshaped.

Quills are available at art shops, as are cane or reed pens. These produce a jerky, coarser line, and are suitable for working on drawings that are done on a larger scale.

The dip pen is perhaps the most versatile for the artist. It consists of a holder made from wood or plastic into which a vast range of nibs of different shapes and sizes can be inserted. Nibs range from the extremely fine to the very broad; it is even possible to buy nibs that produce several parallel lines at once, which makes them useful for drawings that are heavily hatched. Sometimes a new nib has trouble accepting ink, in which case a little saliva rubbed onto the nib will solve the problem.

Ink is either waterproof or non-waterproof and both types are available in a wide range of colours. Waterproof ink can be overlaid with washes; it dries with a slightly glossy surface and sits on the paper surface rather than soaking into it. Washes can be overlaid without fear of dissolving the previous layer. Non-waterproof ink perhaps offers greater flexibility. Overworking with washes will dissolve dry ink – indeed, many of the techniques are similar to those used in watercolour. If ink is thick in the bottle it can be diluted by adding a little distilled water.

Ink can be spattered, brushed, sponged and dabbed onto the support using a variety of implements. Liquid concentrated watercolour and liquid acrylic can also be used for drawing, extending the possibilities for making marks still further.

Always work on a fairly smooth surface. A heavy cartridge paper is ideal, as the nib runs across the surface without catching. By varying pressure on the nib and altering the angle of the pen you can alter the thickness of the line. Ink used straight from the bottle gives a consistent tone, so unless a shading technique is used the only way to suggest variations of tone within a line drawing is through the thickness and quality of the line.

While it is possible to make corrections to a pen drawing, they are often unsatisfactory; in many cases it is the correction that ruins the drawing rather than the mistake. Ink can be removed by blotting, then dabbing with damp paper. Non-waterproof inks can be diluted with clean water then blotted away, and dry ink can be scraped away with a sharp blade. It pays to plan: a simple light, soft pencil drawing can be used as a guide for the pen drawing, and the pencil erased when the drawing is finished. To avoid smudging your drawing allow it to dry for several hours before atempting to correct the mistake with an eraser.

A better result will be achieved if you use the pencil drawing as a rough sketch only, redrawing and re-inventing in ink; trying to follow the pencil line exactly will make for a dull drawing with stilted, dead, laboured line. To clean your nib, rinse it in water. This will stop it clogging with ink and will prolong its life.

Although fountain or reservoir pens are only available with a limited range of nibs, they do offer the advantage of not having to be dipped constantly in ink. They can also be carried in the pocket, which makes them ideal for sketching. To prevent clogging, only fill them with non-waterproof ink.

Any brush can be used with ink. Sable or synthetic watercolour brushes are well suited as are Chinese and Japanese brushes, which are capable of producing extremely fine, delicate lines.

### Other drawing media

There are countless technical pens, markers and felt tips on the market that contain both waterproof and non-waterproof inks. Technical pens are essentially linear tools; tone is achieved by dots or hatching. As each pen puts out a consistent thickness of line, so several pens with nibs of a different thickness are needed for drawings with varying line widths. They can produce drawings with a complete tonal range of great depth. As your pens run out of ink they give an inconsistent, broken line. Don't throw these pens away, as they can be put to good use on those areas that require a minimum of work, bringing yet another quality to the drawing.

Technical pens are best used on a smoother surface such as cartridge paper or card. The same principles apply to ballpoint pens, from which the ink flows easily, making them good for sketching. As they are difficult to erase you are forced, for fear of making mistakes, to look closely at the subject and be incisive with any marks that you make.

Markers, felt and fibre-tipped pens come by the thousand, varying in size and colour. A few are water soluble: most are not. The latter can be blended, removed and softened by using correction markers that contain a solvent. Correction markers can also be obtained that contain white paint, thus pushing the possibilities still further.

Markers tend to bleed through the paper, so when using cartridge paper make sure you cannot harm the surface on which it is resting. Alternatively you can work on bleed-proof paper, which is fairly thin and transparent. It is common practice to produce a rough drawing first, place it beneath a sheet of bleed-proof paper and use the rough drawing as a guide.

You can draw with anything that will make a mark; each implement will bring with it its own distinct qualities and characteristics. Some will be easier to use than others, and there are many that do not need to be expensive art shop purchases. Indeed you can make a drawing with a match stick dipped in ink. All drawing media can be used in conjunction with one another. Try a marriage of ink and charcoal or graphite and chalk; the results can be both unexpected and exciting. Experiment with your materials, but above all enjoy using them.

### Erasers

Erasers should not be thought of simply as the means of getting rid of mistakes; they have a far more important roll to play as a drawing aid that is capable of making its own range of marks. Used with a little care and thought the eraser can add interest and surface quality to areas that have been overworked. They can be used to pull out lighter tones from dark areas, crisply pick out highlights and negative shapes, make patterns and soften hard edges.

Erasers tend to be inexpensive so try a few to see their possible effects. You can even cut them to retain sharp or pointed edges or to remove a dirty profile.

The putty eraser is, as its name suggests, soft and malleable. It can be used for cleaning up large areas or moulded to a point to put in highlights. Because it is soft it is kind to the surface of the paper, but it can get dirty very quickly when used with charcoal or on heavy dark pencil work. It is therefore a good idea to keep one rubber to hand for really dirty jobs and another for cleaner, more detailed work. Alternatively, you can buy the larger size and cut off pieces to use for messy work.

The plastic and India-rubber erasers are harder than the soft kneadable type and are more suited for work on smaller areas or for putting crisp, sharp, light lines into areas of tone. The Artgum eraser is best used to clean up unwanted marks on white paper. Erasers can be used in conjunction with an eraser shield – a small flat sheet of metal with a variety of shapes punched out of the metal. When placed over a drawing it is then possible to erase very small areas without disturbing the surrounding drawing.

### Knives and sharpeners

Pencils and thick charcoal are best sharpened with a sharp craft knife or blade. When the blades themselves are sharp they are easy to control and will sharpen all shapes of pencil – unlike the pencil sharpener, which will only sharpen the strip of standard shaped pencils into a very uniform point. A pencil sharpened with a knife keeps its point longer, as the act of sharpening tends to reveal more of the strip. Sandpaper blocks are available to help shape the point, but if a pencil is sharpened correctly these should not be necessary. Sandpaper is best used to sharpen a stick of charcoal. Pencil sharpeners are used to keep a point on graphite sticks, which should be sharpened frequently. If they are allowed to become blunt and round a great deal of sharpening will be needed to restore the point.

The thicker graphite sticks can be kept sharp by using a sandpaper block, or by scribbling the edge of the pencil very hard on concrete or stone, turning the stick all the time until it has a satisfactory point. Conté and chalk can be sharpened using either a knife or sandpaper.

### Fixative

Drawings in pencil, charcoal, chalk and other soft materials that lie on the surface of the support, rather than permeate it, will smudge if rubbed against, so it is prudent to give the drawing a coat of fixative to bind the drawing material to the surface. When working with very soft material such as charcoal you may find it a good idea to fix the drawing periodically as you work; the layer of fixative does change the feel of the paper surface, so use it sparingly. You may also fix that part of the drawing that you are happy with or feel is complete. Once fixed the drawing cannot be modified by erasing, so think ahead.

Aerosol cans are easily used by holding the can 30 cm/12 in away from the drawing and spraying steadily while moving the can across the drawing. Test the spray before you use it on the drawing as occasionally the fixative fails to atomise, and a jet, rather than a spray, is discharged, which could spoil your work.

### Sundry equipment

A good drawing board is essential. Choose a size that is large enough to accommodate the largest sheet of paper you intend using. Few things are as irksome as trying to work on a sheet of paper that is too large for the drawing board. You may find that it makes good sense to have two boards: a smaller, lighter board for working outside; and a larger, heavier board for working inside. Easels can make the drawing process easier but should not be thought of as a necessity.

A drawing board can usually be rested on or against something, be it a pile of books in the home or a convenient gate or fence post outside. Some artists secure a length of canvas webbing to the middle of each short side of a drawing board; the webbing can then be passed over the head and worn around the neck, supporting the board against the body. Professional artists often have more than one easel, as different easels fulfil very different needs and functions, and it may take time to assess exactly what your own personal needs are. A good easel is a large investment but one that should last a lifetime.

All artists tend to be magpies, picking up more implements and equipment than they need, and the range of materials available is vast. That said, try only to buy what you need; bear in mind that all art shops are notoriously seductive places and that art materials are not cheap.

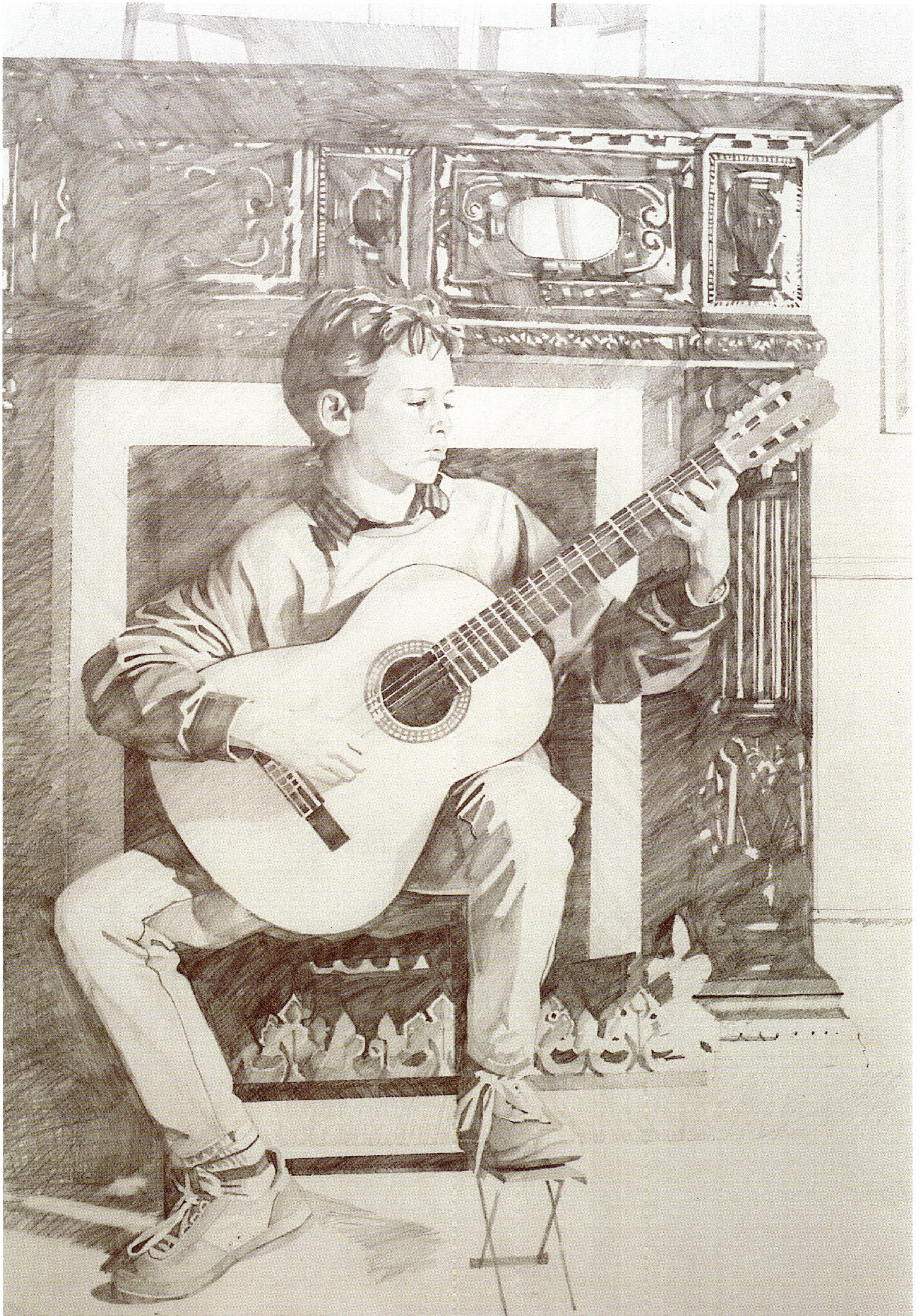

# TECHNIQUES

TECHNIQUES ARE THOSE marks and effects that can be achieved with a chosen medium. Working without some knowledge of the effects that are possible and how to achieve them is really like trying to write a book without having any knowledge of grammar. Think of techniques as a visual vocabulary; being able to call on and be familiar with a repertoire of techniques frees the artist to concentrate on the content of the picture.

Many drawing techniques are remarkably simple, but to use them successfully you need to execute them effortlessly and smoothly. All the best drawings, regardless of style, seem to have been executed with a fluid, easy economy of line, or a combination of marks that seem just right for conveying successfully the artist's vision. While it is true that great or even good art cannot be born of technique alone, a familiarity with materials and the marks that are possible with those materials will certainly bring that vision closer to realisation.

I believe that any time spent handling, experimenting, doodling and scribbling with materials and media will help you acquire the technical skills drawing requires. It is not obligatory or even desirable to have an image in mind. Working abstractly in this way means that you can put more thought and concentration into making the marks. Unconscious control of the drawing media enables us to concentrate on form, perspective, composition, colour and other fundamental underlying principles that are central to good drawing.

Learning about technique is cumulative; as you will see, many of the same techniques are used with several different media. Using and becoming familiar with one technique in one medium will help you when using the same or a similar technique with another.

The techniques that follow are but a selection of the great many that are possible with the range of materials we are using. As you experiment you will discover other drawing materials and ways of making marks for yourself – some by accident. The possibilities are endless. Try working and practising the techniques in a sketch book, or, if the work is done on pieces of scrap paper, paste the results into the sketch book. In this way a very useful visual reference library of possibilities can be built up, to which you can easily refer.

## The Techniques

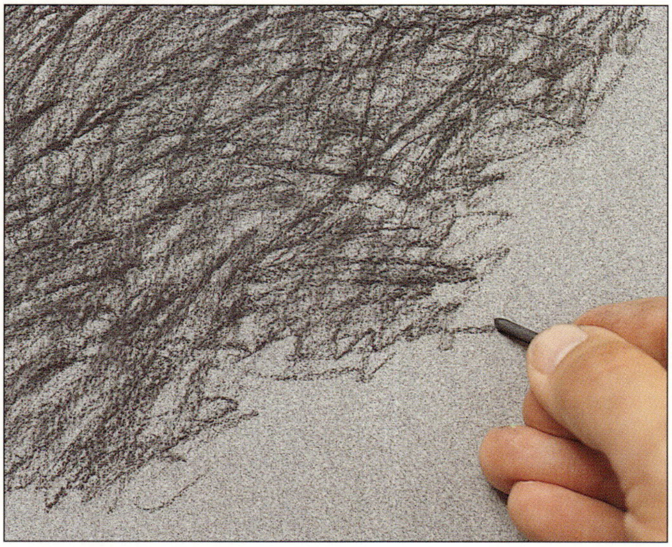

Scribbling with charcoal creates subtle areas of tone of varying density and strength. Large, uniform areas of tone can look flat and uninteresting, whereas scribbled areas varying in density look fresher. They can be built up by covering an area several times over – using the charcoal with more or less the same pressure – or by applying heavier pressure to achieve a thick dark mark. Hold the charcoal nearer the end when using heavier pressure, or the stick will shatter. Holding the stick higher forces you to apply less pressure and so make lighter marks.

Once an area, or patch, of scribbled tone has been laid it can be blended to a smoother finish by using tissue, a soft cloth, torchon or finger. If using a finger

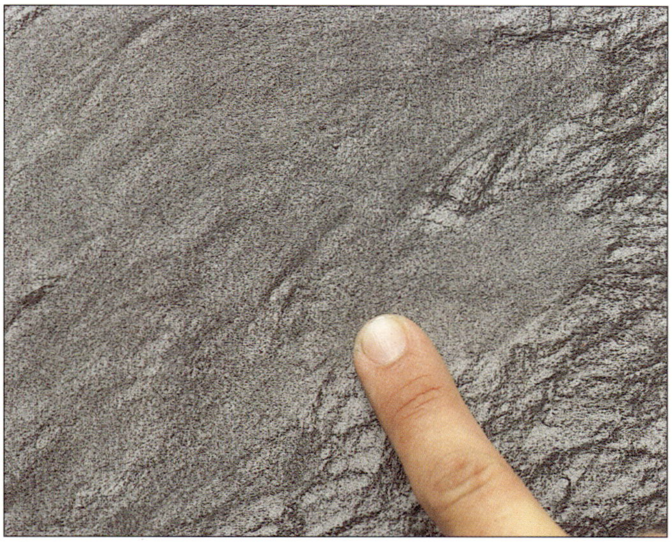

make sure it is dry and rub lightly, blending the marks; repeating the process of scribbling and blending will give a darker tone. If you intend to blend an area in this way do not press too hard with the charcoal, as once embedded in the paper it will become increasingly difficult to blend successfully. To build a dark enough tone it may be necessary to apply some fixative between layers.

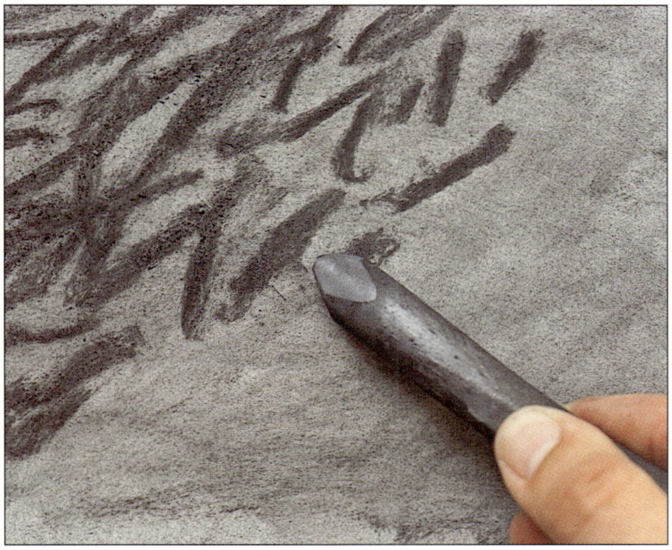

You can work over a light area of charcoal with a variety of marks made with more charcoal (or chalk). As the thickness of charcoal dust builds on the paper surface a point will be reached when the drawing will need to be fixed before it will accept any more charcoal; otherwise the stick will slide over and remove some of what is already there.

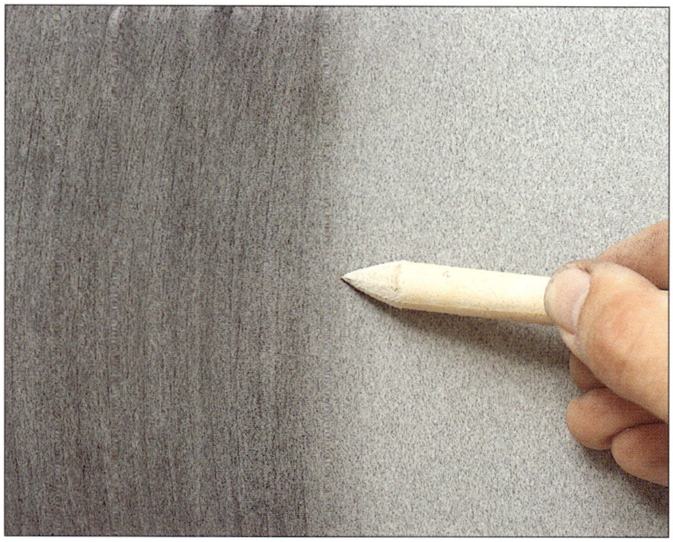

To achieve a subtle and gradual change in tone the charcoal is applied loosely and then blended with a torchon. Charcoal is not applied to the lightest area, but the charcoal powder is pulled with the torchon across the surface of the paper into the light areas. A finger, tissues, clean rags or cotton wool buds can be used, but the torchon, because of its shape, is ideal for the purpose, making it possible to blend in very small confined areas as well as over more open, larger expanses of drawing. It is also possible to draw with the torchon simply by picking up charcoal dust on the end and rubbing it onto the paper.

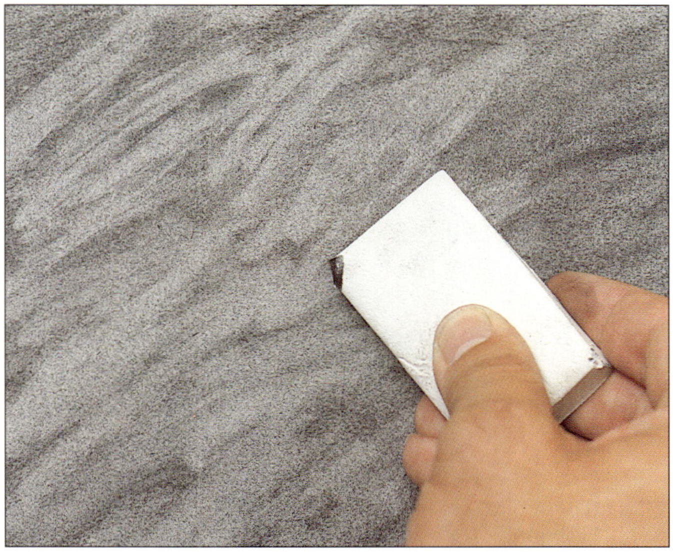

The eraser plays an important role when drawing. Not only is it a means of correcting mistakes, it is also used to draw into areas of laid charcoal, pencil, conté or any other soft medium. Large areas of flat tone can be lightened or given texture, and lines can be drawn or redefined and highlights flicked in. The kneadable putty erasers are well suited to charcoal: the harder plastic erasers tend to push the charcoal deep into the paper. Try a selection with different media. The eraser will get dirty quickly and once covered in thick charcoal will not work as well. Use a sharp knife to cut away the dirty portion, revealing the clean eraser beneath. Harder erasers can be sliced at an angle to keep a sharp edge; soft erasers can also be shaped to a point either by pulling or by cutting with a sharp knife. When lifting out small highlights do not rub with the eraser – just press down hard and lift the charcoal from the surface.

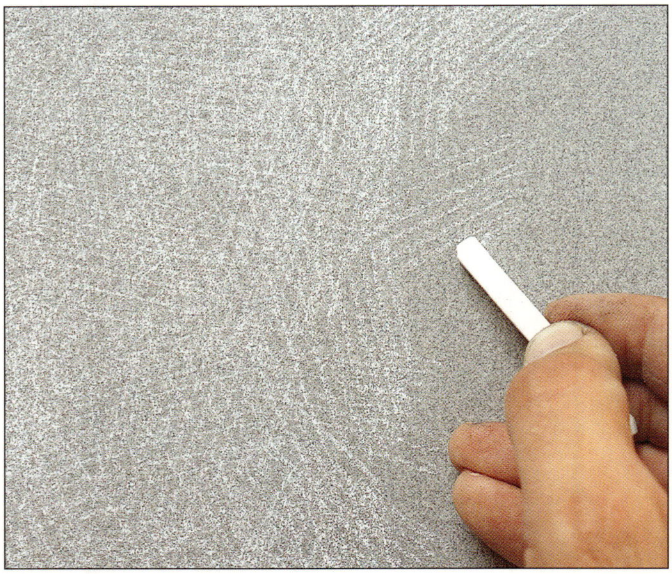

▲ With the softer materials tone is easily built up by blending: with harder materials this becomes more difficult, so line is used. By cross-hatching lines of varying density or thickness it is possible to achieve a complete tonal range. The technique is used with soft materials too but the effect is less satisfactory than when it is done with those drawing materials capable of making crisper marks; here, white conté is used. Cross-hatching is a very controllable way to render light and shade; it can be slow and considered or fast and loose. The lines do not have to be straight but can curve into the contours of your image, helping to suggest the form.

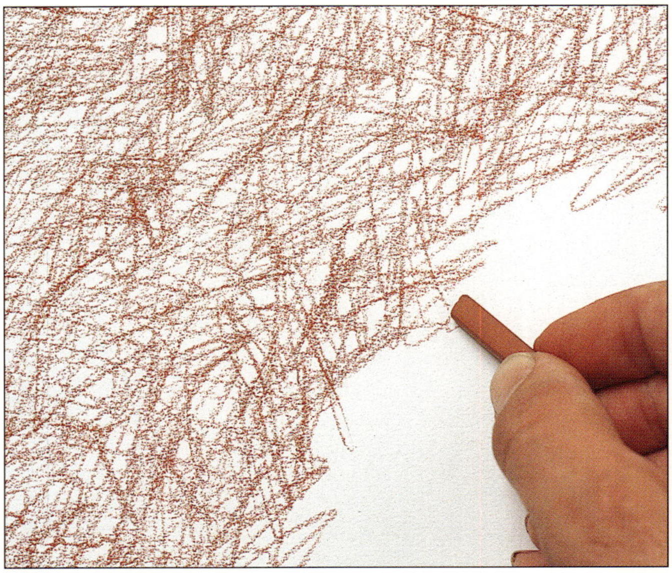

▲ Scribbling with conté, like charcoal, enables you to build tone gradually over large areas while keeping an interesting surface. The areas of support that are left showing between the marks – in this case white paper – are as important as the marks themselves; it is the balance between the marks and the paper that gives the desired density. Varying the direction of the strokes, as with hatching, ensures that the observer's eye is led in more than one direction.

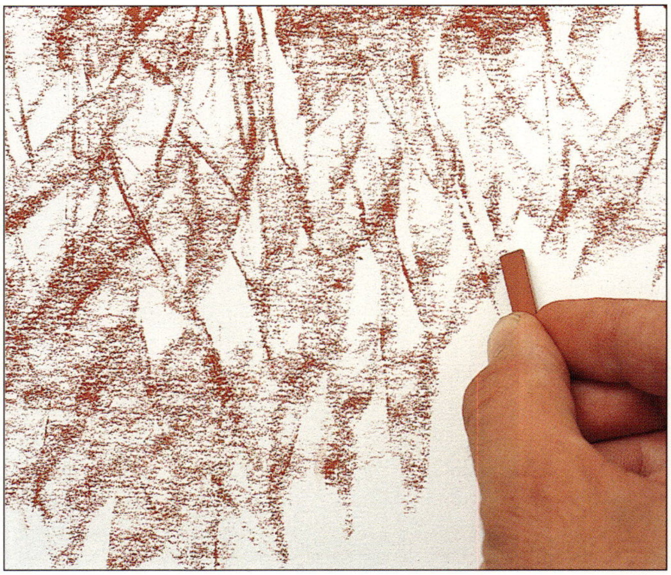

▲ With drawing materials such as charcoal or conté sticks that have a large marking surface, it is possible to utilise the whole stick. Here the sharp, long edge of a conté stick is pulled up and down in an inverted 'V', while at the same time it is moved sideways.

By working in layers you can achieve effects that would otherwise be impossible. The surface of an area of sanguine conté – blocked in by using the stick on its side – is fixed, then given added interest by lightly

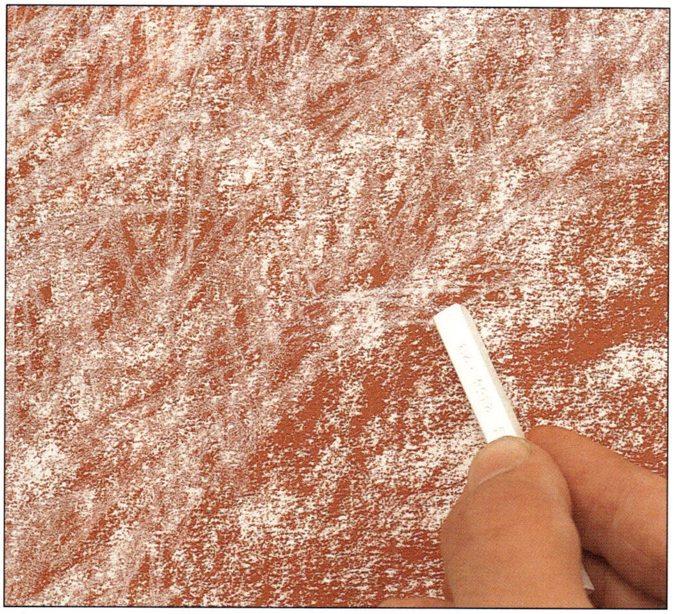

scribbling over the surface with the end of a stick of white conté.

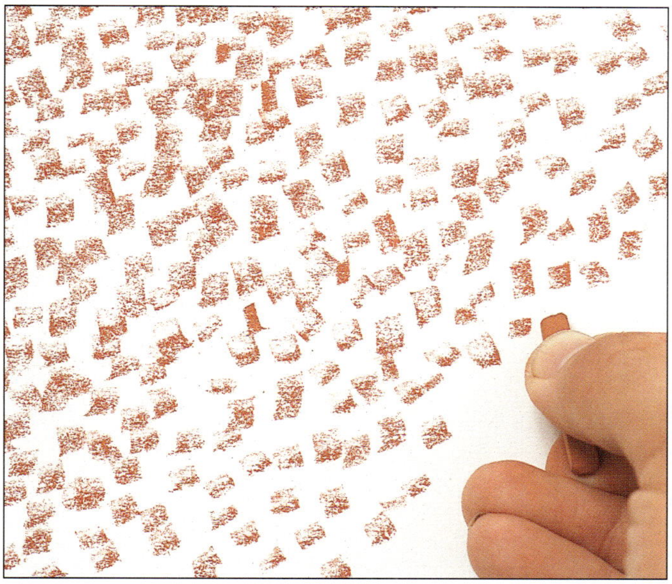

Building areas of texture and tone by dotting or stippling can take time. However it is a useful technique that can be used in conjunction with others to give added interest. The blunt, square end of a conté stick can be used to make short or long marks. The suggestion of tone is made by varying the density of the dots and therefore the amount of white paper showing around them.

If a sheet of paper is placed over a firm textured surface, such as floorboards or a metal grill, and a soft

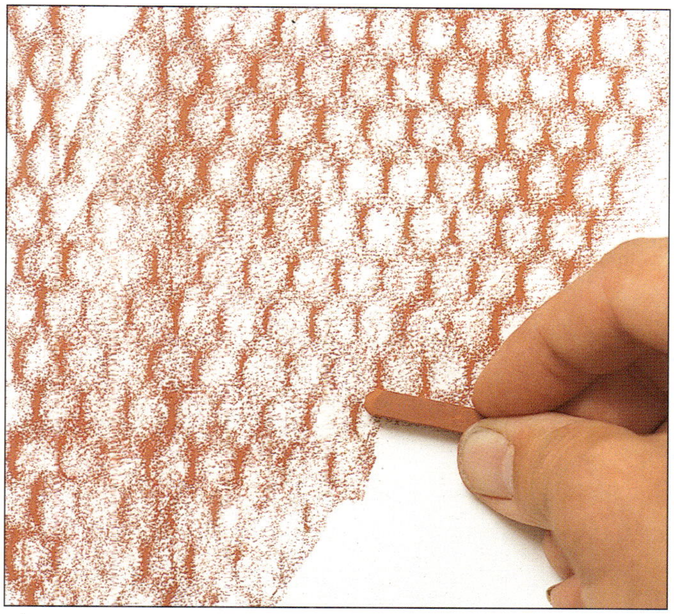

drawing implement is rubbed over the paper surface, an image of the texture will show through. This is known as *frottage*, which can be a useful technique to have in the repertoire. While it is not necessarily used on its own to make a drawing, it can be used in conjunction with other techniques to give variety and relief to an image.

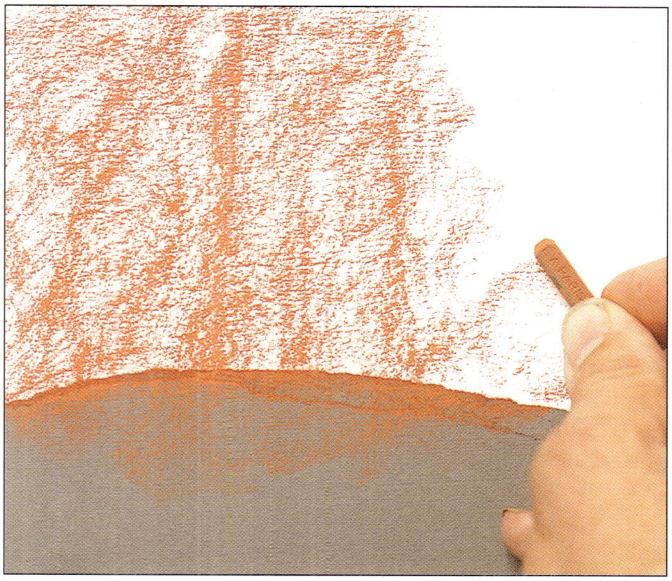

To work up to an edge with an area of tone and give that edge a distinct quality, a piece of paper torn or cut to shape can be placed on the drawing to act as a mask. Holding the mask carefully so that it does not slip, the drawing medium – in this case a sanguine conté stick – is worked over the desired area and the edge of the mask.

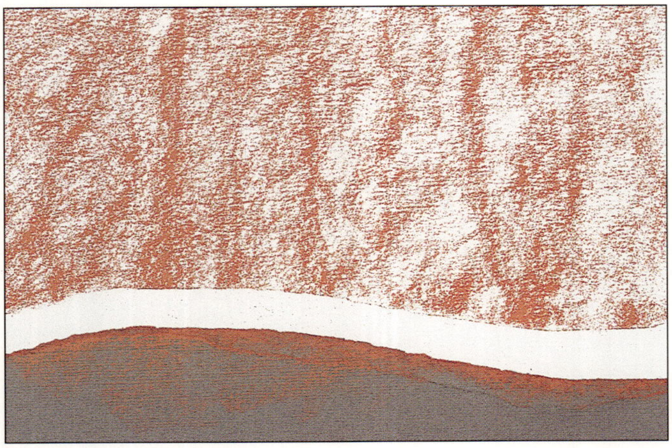

When the mask is removed you will be left with a line that is difficult to achieve by other means.

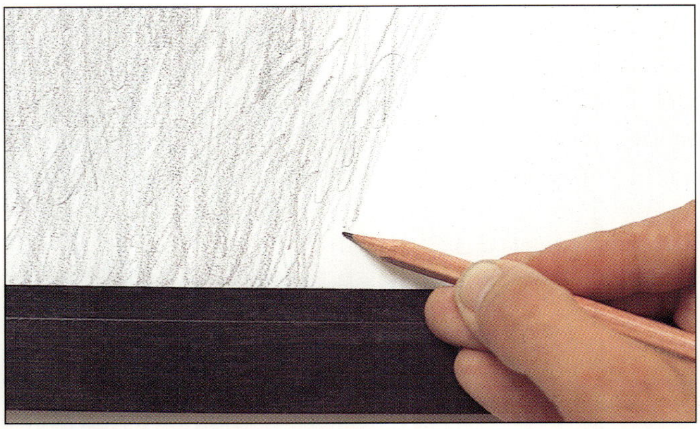

With harder drawing materials such as pencils and graphite sticks that tend to have a point, a similar result can be achieved by using a thicker material, such as a piece of card or a ruler, as a mask.

The mask needs to be thick because the point tends to catch on thinner materials, pulling them up or even tearing them.

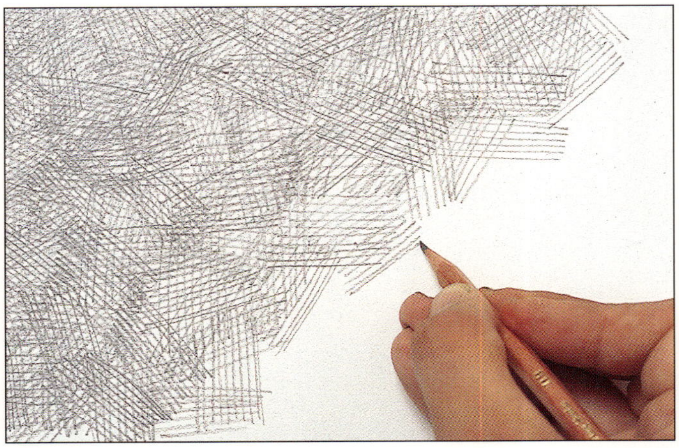

A sharp pencil hatches and cross-hatches beautifully; a mix of hard and soft grades produces a full range of tones from an almost imperceptible light grey to deep black. While it is possible to get a range of tone with a single pencil by pressing harder, do not try to get a dark tone with a hard pencil – you will only succeed in making deep indentations. If you require a darker tone choose a softer grade pencil.

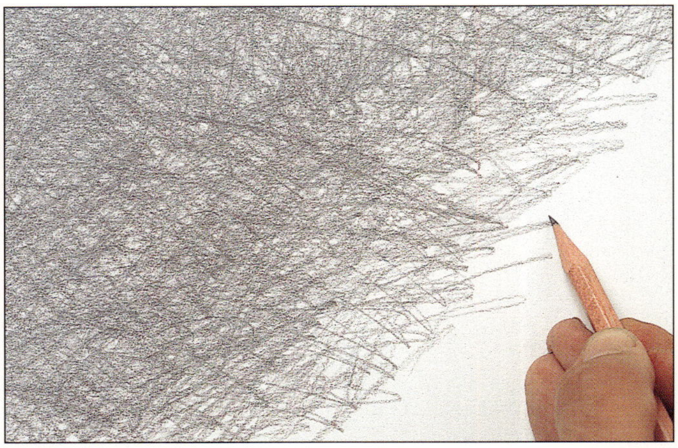

Scribbling with a pencil is a quick way of laying down an area of tone or texture. As with charcoal you will find that holding the pencil higher up the shaft will enable you to achieve a lighter, uniform tone, while holding the pencil further down – closer to the point – will enable you to apply greater pressure and so make darker marks. Remember to vary the direction of your strokes.

Graphite powder is sprinkled onto the surface sparingly and then blended and rubbed into the surface with a finger or soft cloth. Any excess powder can be tipped back into the jar. The depth of tone achievable is limited, and the powder, once spread, does have a

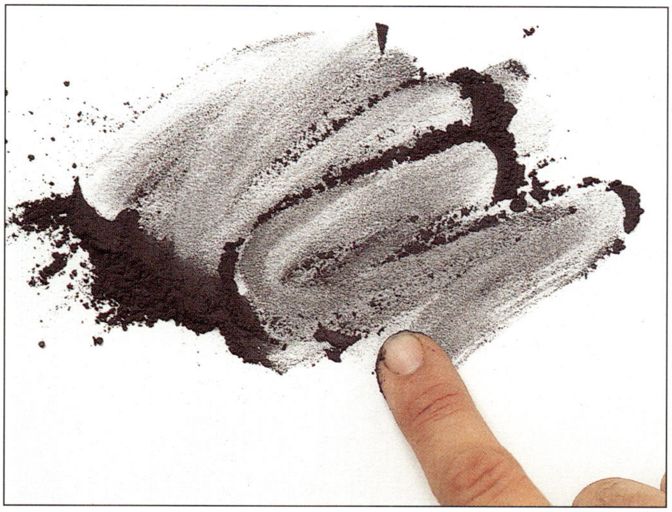

▲ tendency to look flat. To achieve darker tones you will have to fix one layer and then overlay another; detail can be drawn with a torchon dipped into the powder. The secret is to work loosely and use the technique in conjunction with others. Keep the surface alive with soft-pencil work and work into it with the eraser; this will have to be done before the work is fixed. Fix well once the powder has been used, as, like charcoal, it will smudge off onto anything that rubs against it.

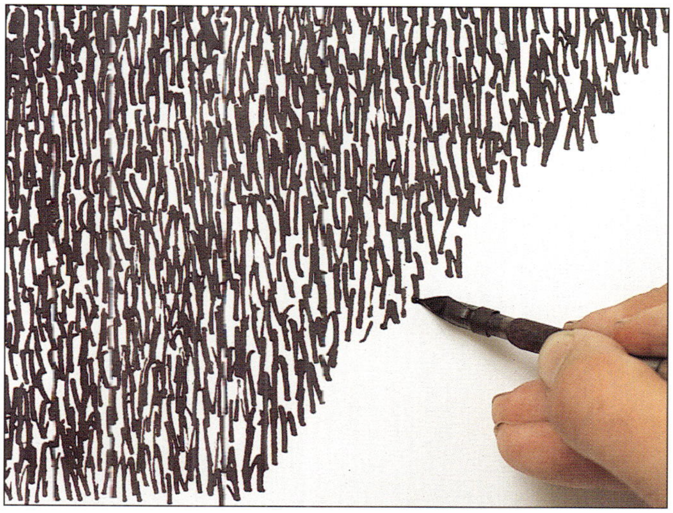

▲ Calligraphy nibs give a greater range of thickness to line than standard dip pen nibs. Drawings can be made using a single nib that, because of its shape, is able to produce a single line of varying thickness. This is accomplished not by pressure but by altering the angle of the nib to the paper. While not as versatile as the standard nib, a calligraphy nib could be put to good use in conjunction with a standard nib to give a drawing a greater range of line quality.

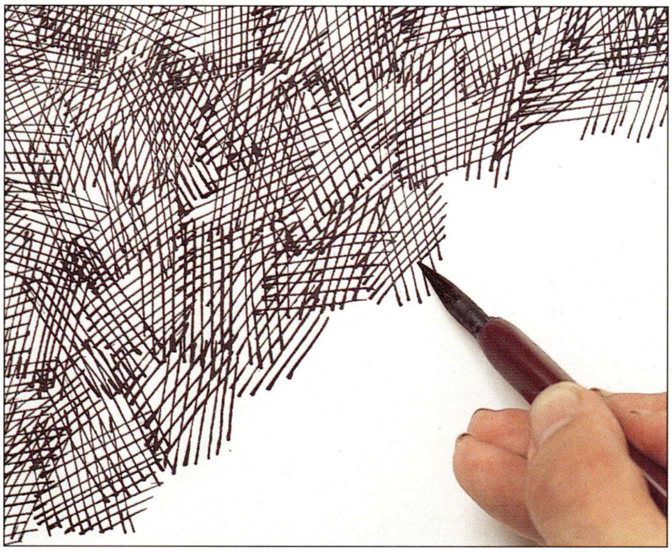

▲ The dip pen is essentially a tool for making lines; cross-hatching in ink is crisp, and when handled well can be very effective. A single nib can produce hatching with lines of a regular thickness, tone being suggested by their density; by applying more pressure the lines can be made to vary in thickness. Alternatively you can change to a thicker or thinner nib to give the line produced greater variety.

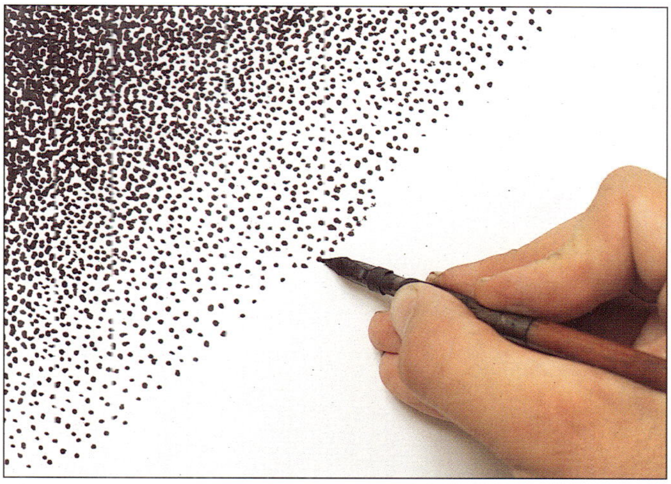

▲ Uniform black dots placed close together appear darker than those placed further apart: the principle is the same as cross-hatching. The process is slow and can look mechanical but is capable of achieving very gradual gradations across the tonal scale. Be careful not to make a blot as this will spoil the subtle effect. Any nib can be used: here the particular shape of a calligraphy nib gives a precise dot. Technical pens and fine liners are an ideal choice for dot drawings. These are available in a range of nib sizes and deliver a steady flow of ink that will not blob.

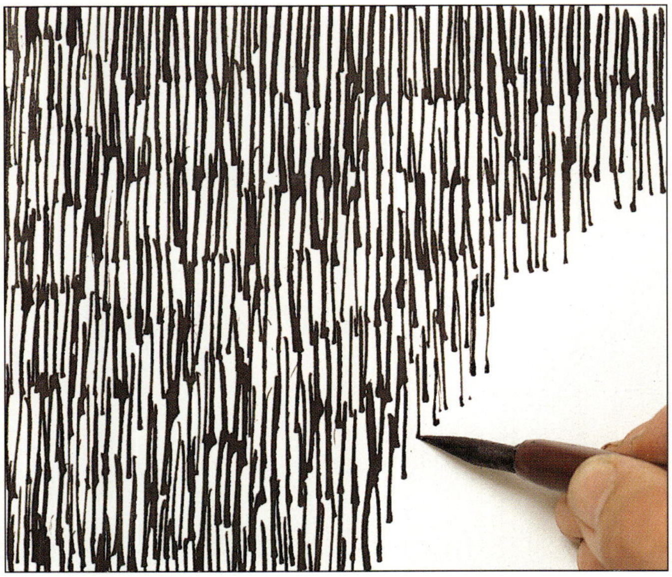

Hatching with a dip pen can be done in any direction to describe form texture and tone. As with other dip pen techniques line variety is brought about by pressure, line density and thickness suggesting tone. The technique is quick to do but requires care and thought, as a drawing produced with lines hatched in one direction only can look lop-sided, as the eye is drawn in the direction that the hatched lines are running.

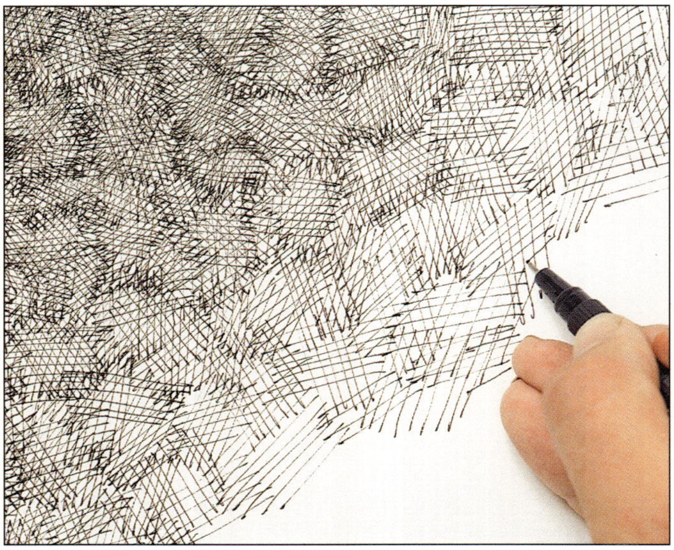

Cross-hatching with a fine liner or technical pen gives a uniform line thickness and can look mechanical and flat; however, because the nib is thin and the flow of ink steady, the results can be very subtle. You cannot change the thickness of the line by pressure, so if you require variety in the thickness of your line you will need a range of pens with nibs of varying sizes.

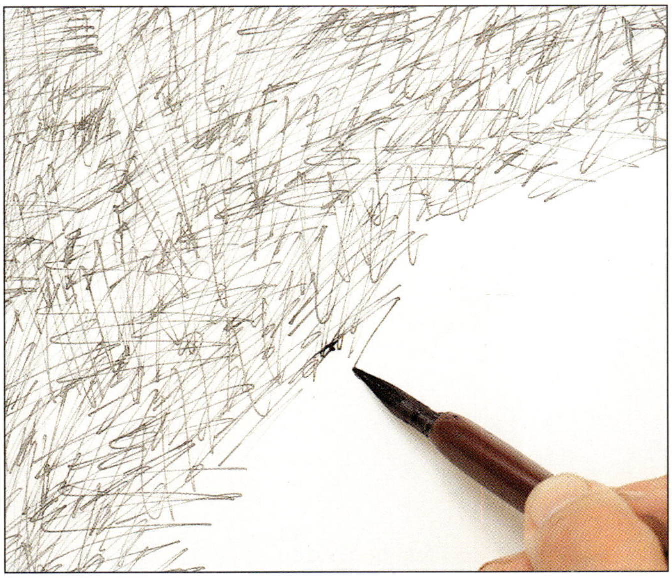

Scribbling with a dip pen can take some getting used to. Tone can be built up in the same way as cross-hatching; although the principle is the same, the finished effect has a more spontaneous and lively look. The ink can be diluted with water to give a grey rather than a black line, as shown here. Diluting the ink alters its viscosity, making it thinner and more prone to run from the nib, so add the dilute ink to the nib with a brush, a little at a time.

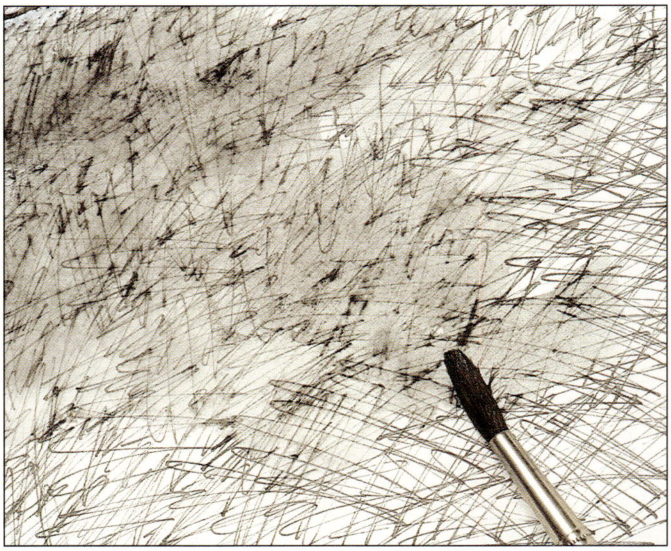

If non-waterproof ink has been used, brushing over the work with clean water when it is dry will dissolve the ink, making it possible to lighten pen work, soften lines and modify tones. The drawing can be overworked again with pen and the process repeated. Make sure the drawing is completely dry before working in layers, or the pen will stick into and pull at the fibres of the paper. Interesting and useful effects can be achieved by using a mixture of waterproof and non-waterproof inks in layers. When water, dilute ink or watercolour is brushed on, the dry waterproof ink will stay stable and any lines crisp.

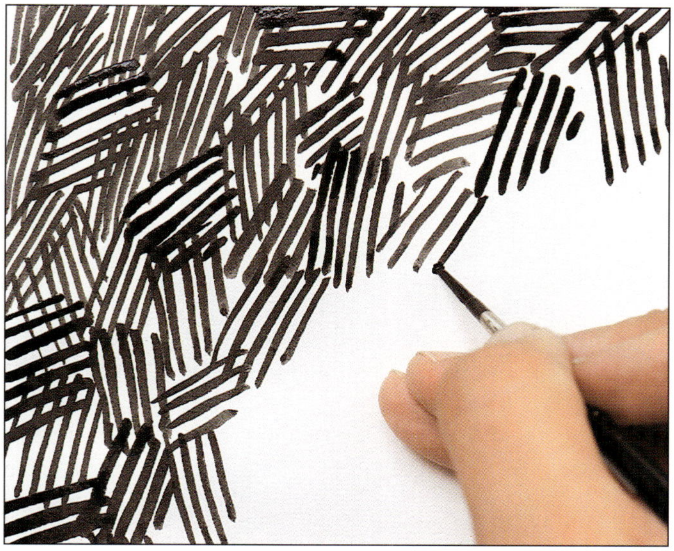

Lines can be drawn with a brush of any thickness; soft watercolour brushes are ideal but you can also try larger bristle brushes – the trick is to work confidently. Hesitant work will show in the quality of the marks. Take care not to smudge your drawing: the ink, when applied thickly from a brush, can take hours to dry. You can dilute the ink with water to give a lighter, more subtle line.

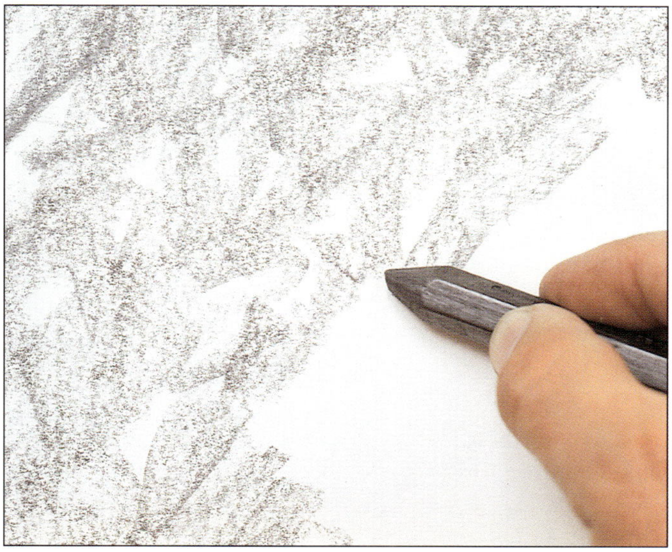

The shape of a graphite pencil allows for a wider range of marks to be made than is possible with an ordinary pencil. Using the pencil on its side enables large expanses of tone to be blocked in very quickly. They are the ideal sketching tool when speed is needed to capture the moment.

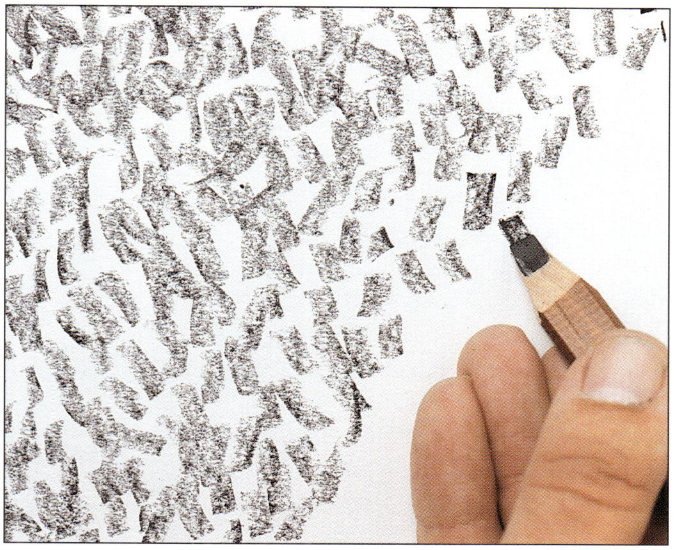

Studio pencils and graphite sticks can lay in areas of tone faster than the standard pencil because of the flattened strip. Here short, broad marks using the full width of the pencil are made. However by turning the pencil on its side (so that the narrowest part of the point is in contact with the paper), you alter the angle at which the graphite strip comes into contact with the paper, thus varying the width of the mark.

# A HOUSEPLANT

*Pencil*

PROJECT ONE

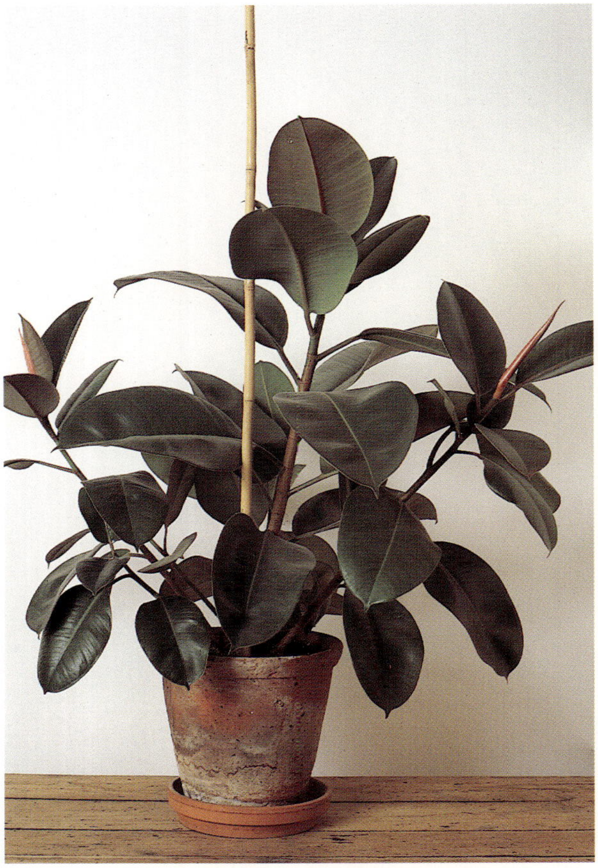

REGARDLESS OF THE size at which you choose to work, and regardless of the medium you choose, the ability to draw accurately relies on being able to assess proportion, position and structure correctly. By using a combination of measurement and vertical and horizontal plumb lines, and by reading negative space correctly, the position and structure of your subject can be transferred to your drawing. The details can be addressed later – the correct shape of objects and their relationship to each other must come first.

The distance between two points can be measured by holding a pencil at arm's length, closing one eye and sighting along the outstretched arm, past the pencil and on to the subject. The top, or end, of the pencil is visually positioned against one point on the subject (for example, the top of the plant pot); the thumb is then moved up the shaft of the pencil to mark the other point (for example the base of the plant pot), thus giving a unit of measurement. Then, keeping the thumb in the same position, the pencil is held against the paper and the measurement marked off.

These measured points are usually placed where a line changes direction or is intersected by another line. By taking just a few preliminary measurements in this way you can plot and position your drawing on the paper and check for accuracy as it develops. If you decide to work on a smaller or larger scale then the unit of measurement indicated on the drawing is adjusted accordingly: by doubling the unit the drawn image will be twice the size; by halving the unit of measurement the drawing will be half the size. The important thing is to keep your measurements, calculations and position they are taken from consistent. Plumb lines dropped vertically and lines run across the drawing horizontally, when used together with measuring, help position objects and elements relative to one another.

Negative spaces are those spaces or shapes that surround the positive forms or objects that you are drawing. Logic will tell you that getting the negative shapes right means the positive shapes are also right; the way they relate is critical and a good means of judging the accuracy of your drawing. Negatives also play an important role in composition, acting as a balance to the positive, more obvious shapes.

A rubber plant is the perfect subject to practice measuring and accuracy. The leaves are large and relatively simple in shape, giving good negative spaces around and between. Work with a HB or softer pencil on a sheet of medium weight A2 cartridge paper secured to a drawing board and held vertically on an easel or propped up on a chair. Position the easel so you only need to turn slightly to face your subject.

## MATERIALS AND EQUIPMENT

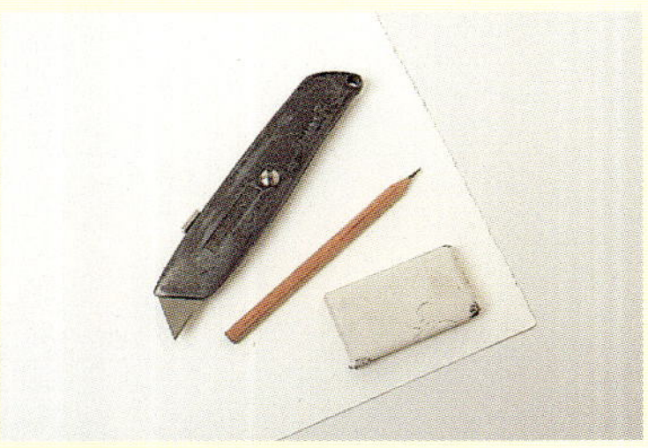

- Sheet of A2 paper
- Stanley knife or craft knife
- HB pencil
- Putty eraser

# The Drawing

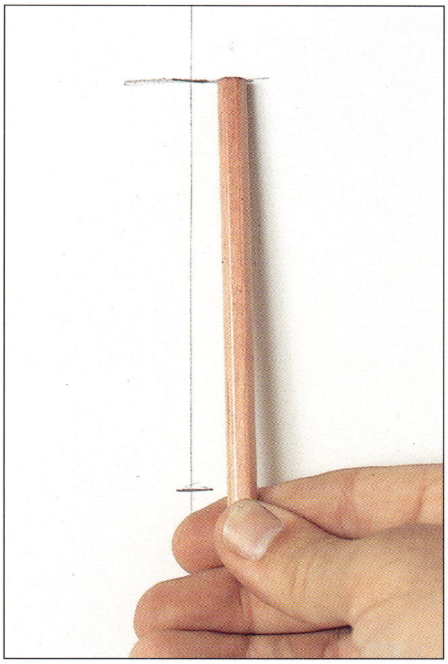

1 To find a convenient unit of measurement, hold your pencil upright at arm's length, close one eye and look past the pencil to the plant. In this case the measurement used is the distance between the first and second notches on the bamboo stake. Applying this unit of measurement, it is calculated that from the first notch on the stake to the bottom of the flower pot is four-and-a-half units. and that from the outer leaf on one side across the plant to the other side is three-and-a-half units.

2 Conveniently, the bamboo stake is more or less vertical, so a line representing the position of the stake is dropped down the sheet of paper slightly off-centre. Against this, beginning a little away from the top edge of the paper, the four-and-a-half units giving the height of the plant and pot are marked. Half way down the vertical line a horizontal line is drawn; against this the three-and-a-half units of measurement are marked – one-and-a-half units on one side of the vertical and two units on the other side of the vertical, giving the width of the plant and indicating that the major part of the plant falls on the side that measures two units.

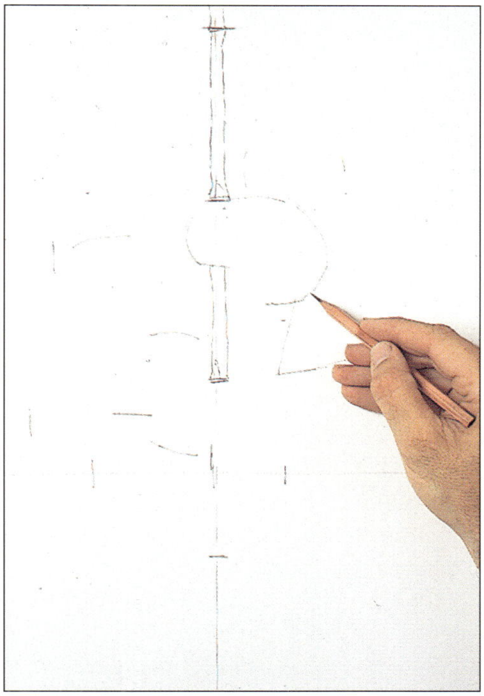

3 With the overall proportions plotted, and in the knowledge that all of the plant will fit onto the paper, the top of the bamboo stake is drawn disappearing off the top of the sheet of paper, and the position of the leaves relative to the stake can begin to be indicated. The leaf positions are measured and plotted in the same way as the overall position of the plant, by using the pencil to measure distances and transferring those measurements onto the drawing. Mark the measurements lightly if you do not want them to show when the drawing is complete; however these marks can add interest to a drawing, showing, as they do, how it was constructed.

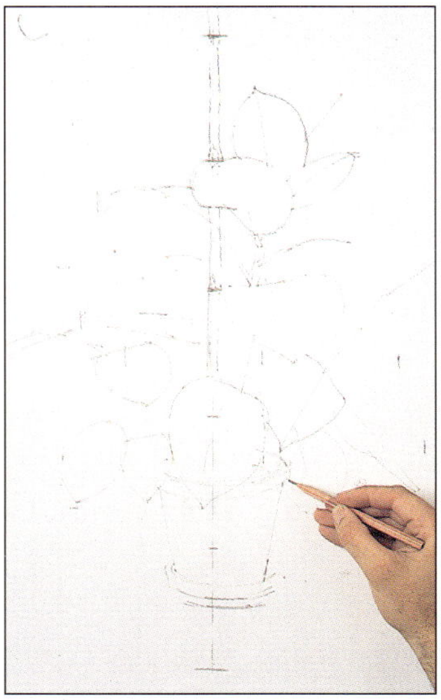

4 As the drawing progresses, the job does become relatively easier, as there is more of a drawn image to which you can relate your new measurements. Where a line runs at an angle the position of the line is calculated by taking horizontal and vertical measurements that mark the position of each end of the line. The two marks are then joined, giving the correct angle.

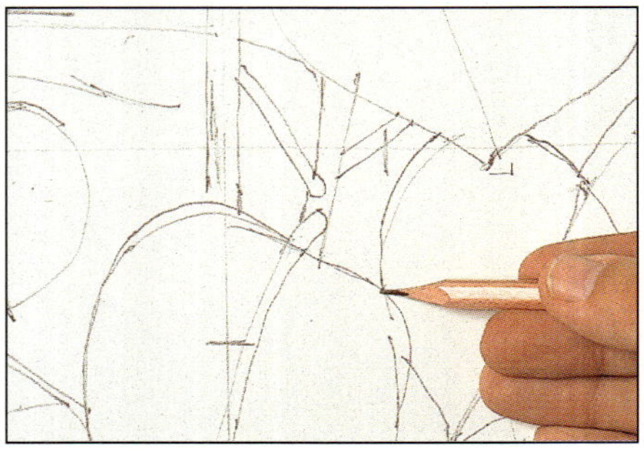

5 When a framework of relative positions is established the drawing process becomes freer; the position of lines and the point at which they intersect other lines can be calculated visually without the need to take measurements. An awareness of the negative shapes between and around the leaves will enable you to check the drawing for accuracy.

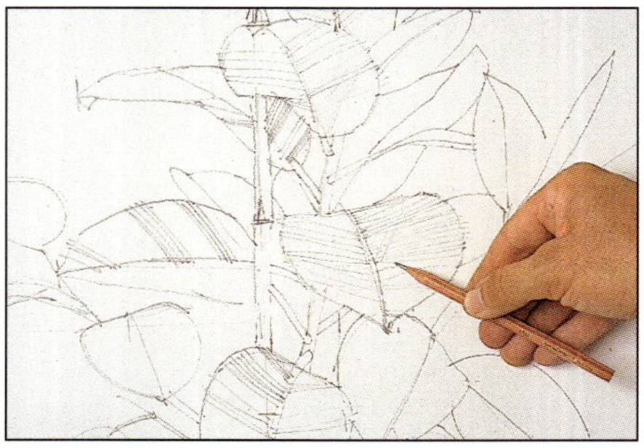

6 The shape of the plant has been described so far in line only: we have concentrated on getting the proportion and position right. The angles and internal contours are now hinted at by working into the leaves with line, indicating the veins and ridges. These help us read the direction and way the leaves hang from the main stem. These internal contour lines combine with the outline drawing to give the plant form.

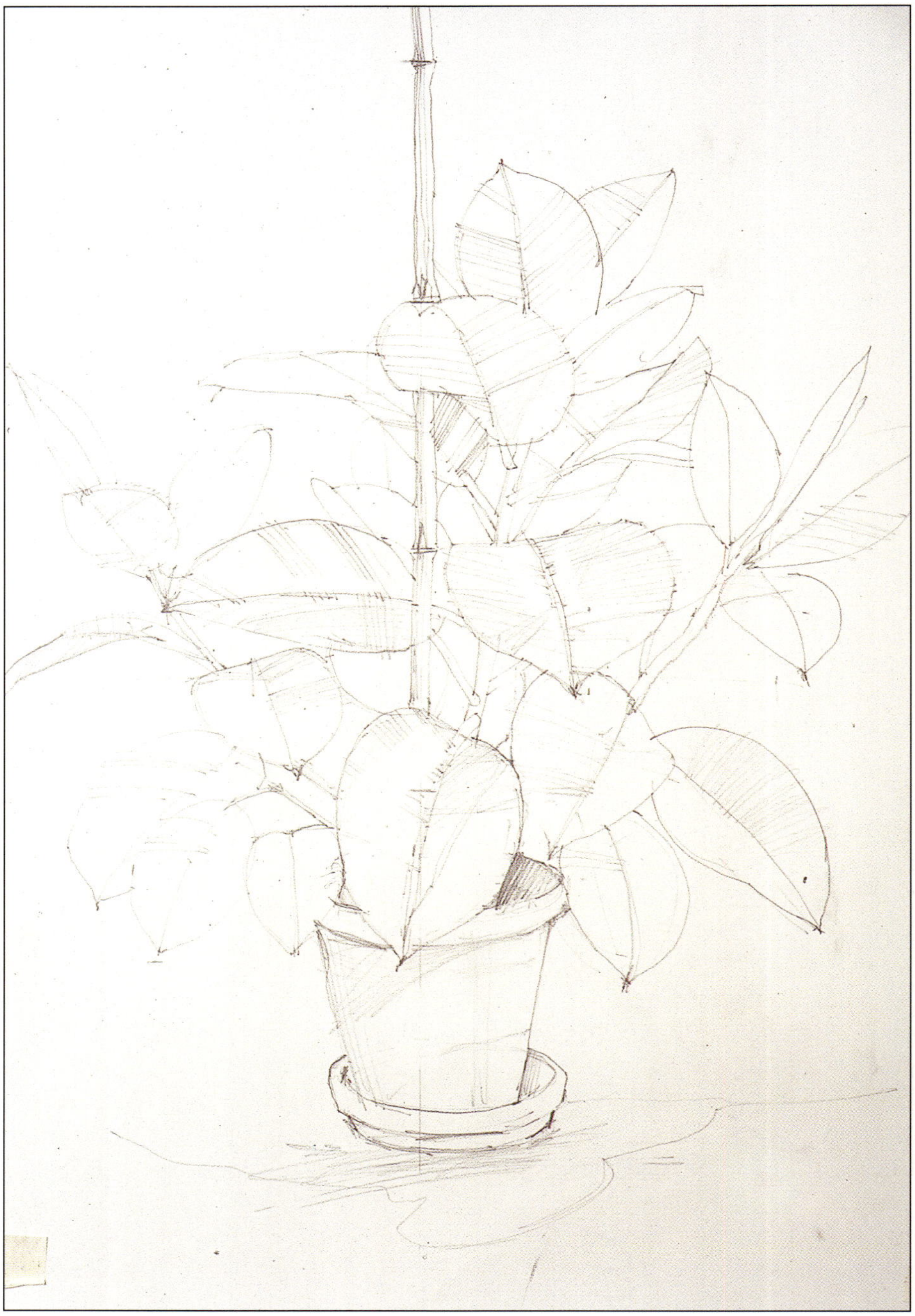

7 The simple drawing is completed with a little loose dark shading on the inside of the flower pot, which helps to push forward the large leaf that is hanging in front, and hints at the pot's roundness. A few lines run down one side of the cane serves the same purpose, helping the viewer read it as a round, three-dimensional, shape rather than as a flat, two-dimensional shape.

# Alternative Approaches

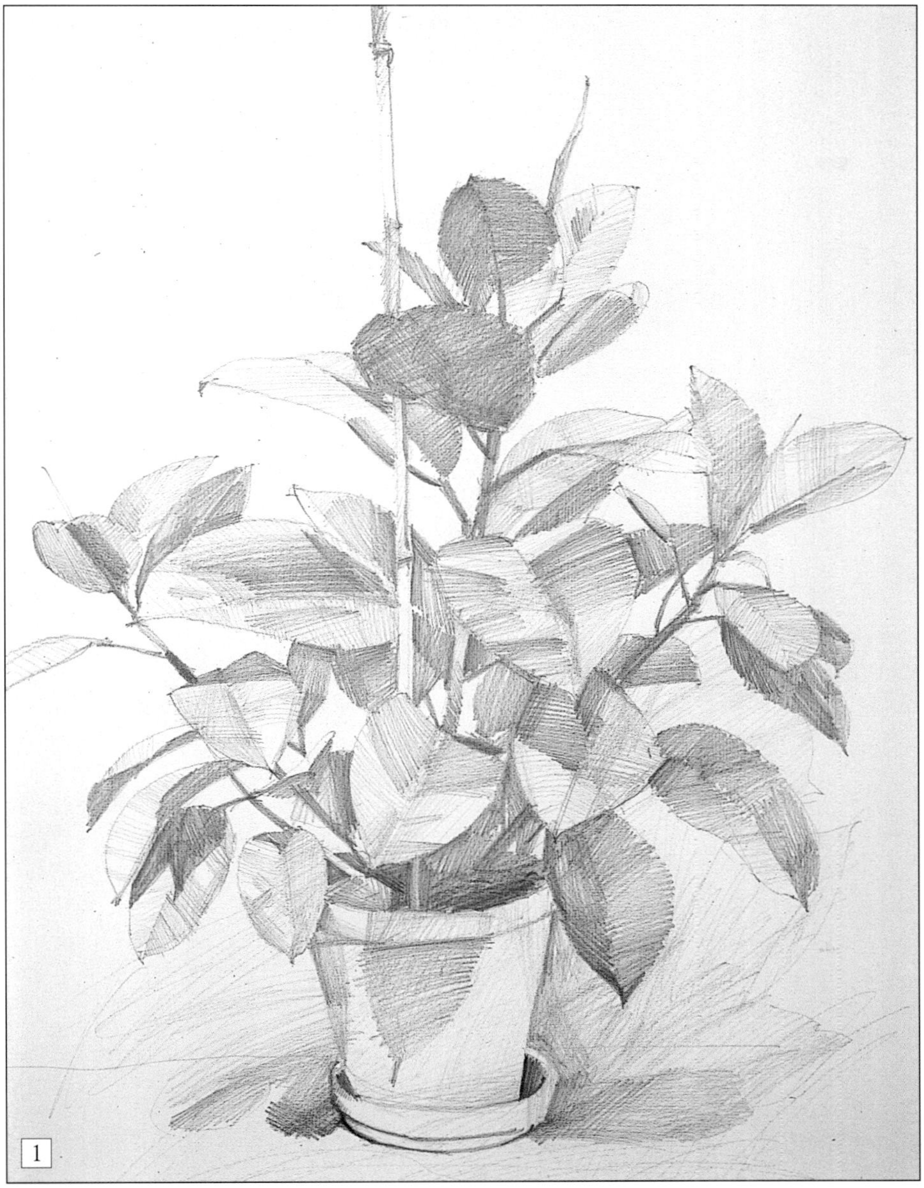

1

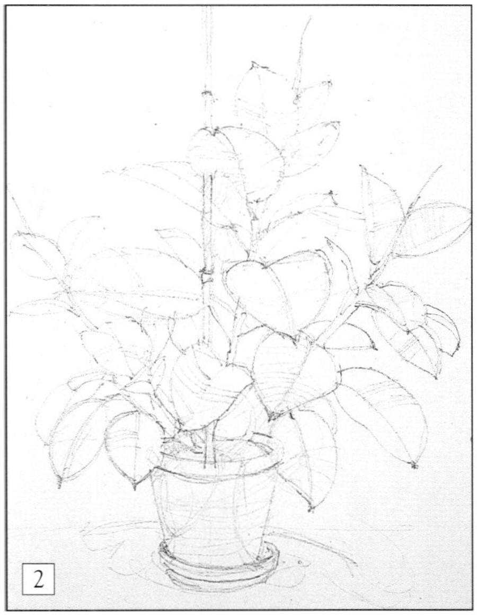

2

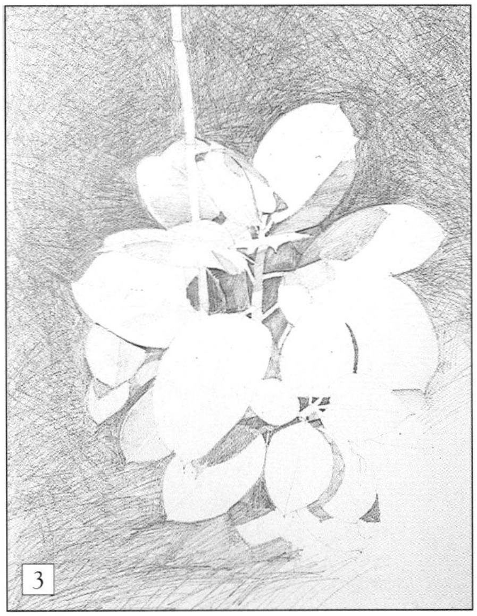

3

**1** Once the structure and shape of the plant were established in light pencil, tone was hatched and scribbled, giving the plant form and dimension. The shading is simple, lively and directional, following the planes of the leaves and suggesting their angle and position relative to each other.

**2** In this drawing a soft graphite pencil was used to explore and search out the shape and contours of the plant. Once a few guidelines had been indicated to keep the drawing on track the pencil was kept moving over the surface of the paper, defining and redefining the shapes, working in and around them. This approach gives the drawing a fluid, lyrical quality.

**3** By changing the viewpoint and looking down on the plant the pot disappears and the leaves become larger, flatter shapes. By concentrating on the dark, negative spaces between and around the leaves they are made to stand out from the background, reaching up and out to the viewer. The scribbled tone over the background, while being a fairly uniform large area, is broken and multi-directional, creating an interesting texture.

# FRUIT AND VEGETABLES

*Pencil*

PROJECT TWO

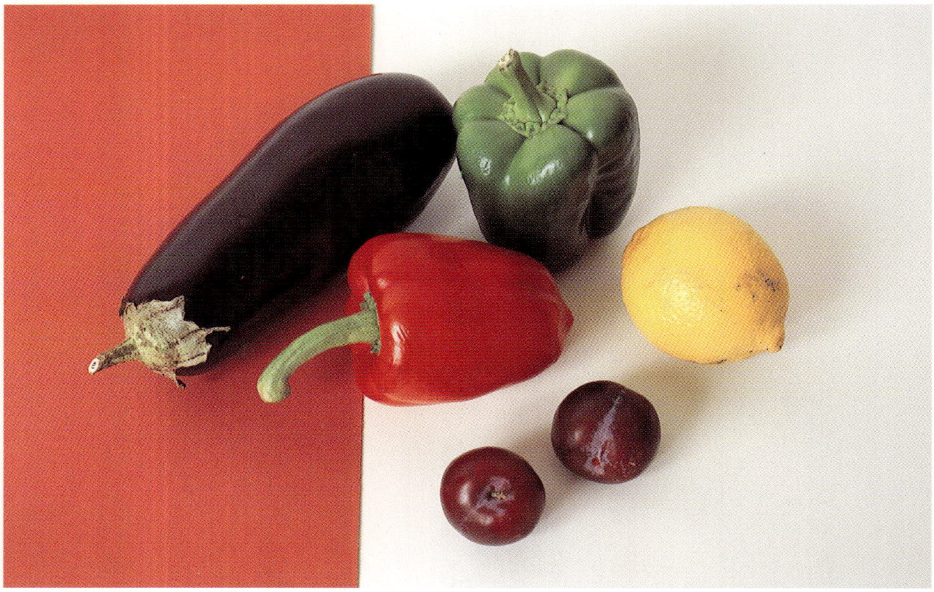

IT IS THE light that falls onto an object that enables us to see that object as a form in three dimensions. That side of an object facing the light source will be the lightest, while the side furthest away or hidden from the light source will be the darkest. To draw an object so that it appears to be three dimensional we need to show these light and dark areas.

This graduation from light to dark is known as a tonal or achromatic scale. The scale runs from white through all the possible shades of grey to black. The principle is simple: putting it into practice can be a little more difficult, as the following exercise illustrates.

With a pencil, draw a circle on a sheet of paper. The circle is all that you see, but if you then work from one side of the circle to the other, scribbling on tone that gets progressively darker as you move across the circle, it will begin to look like a ball or a sphere. The scribbled shading or tone has suggested the form.

Tone is also used to suggest colour. Draw a pair of circles side-by-side on a sheet of paper. Imagine one is a bright yellow ball and the other a dark blue ball. The overall tone you need to use to suggest the colour of the blue ball will be much darker than the overall tone needed for the yellow ball.

Assessing and separating tonal values can be difficult because they are affected and influenced by colour, pattern, texture and the changing intensity or direction of the light source. Looking at your subject through half-closed eyes can help, as this visually simplifies and exaggerates the play of light and shade on the subject – so simplifying and reducing the range of perceived tones.

It is not always necessary or even advisable to try and represent the complete range of tones: an object can be made to look three-dimensional by using only a very dark, a mid and a very light grey tone.

For this project a selection of different shaped coloured fruit and vegetables are used to explore the effects of light on colour and form. The small still life is set up on a sheet of white paper, with a second sheet of red paper positioned about one-third of the way across. The coloured paper serves as an aid to composition, breaking up and adding interest behind the group. Work on an A3 sheet of medium-weight cartridge paper using a 2B pencil. You will need a putty eraser for highlighting and for correcting tone that you consider to be too dark.

## MATERIALS AND EQUIPMENT

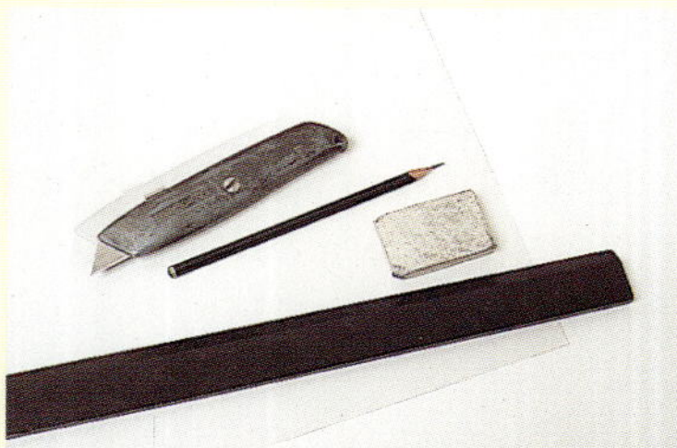

- Sheet of medium-weight A3 paper
- Stanley knife or craft knife
- 2B pencil
- Putty eraser
- Ruler

# The Drawing

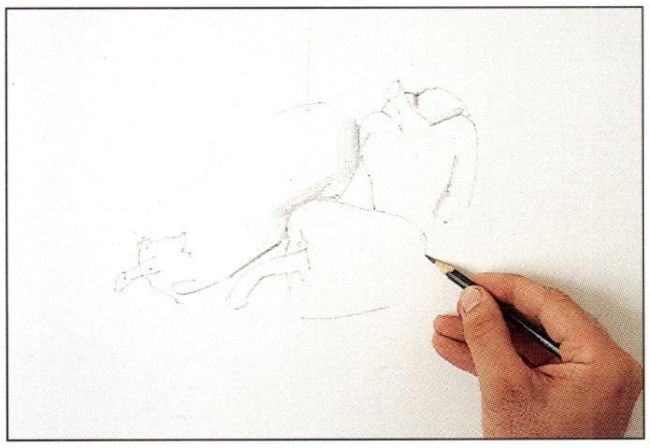

1 Using a 2B pencil establish the position of the aubergine and the two peppers. The position of the red sheet of paper is indicated where it intersects the top of the aubergine. A little tone is scribbled loosely to indicate the edge of the pepper against the dark aubergine. This has the immediate effect of placing the pepper at the front of the group.

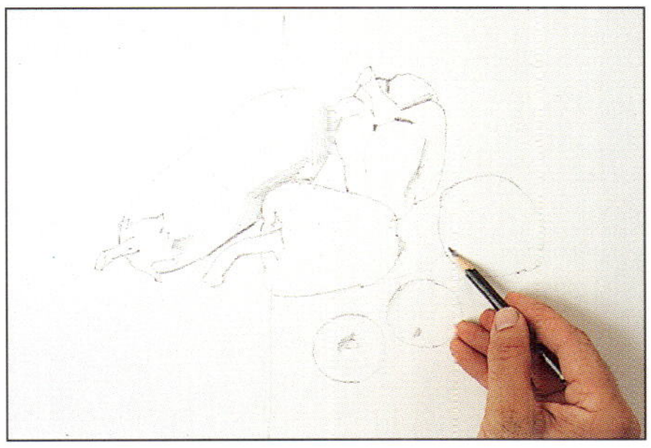

2 The line representing the edge of the dark sheet of paper is continued down from the front pepper. The two plums are positioned at the front of the group before lightly sketching in the lemon on the right.

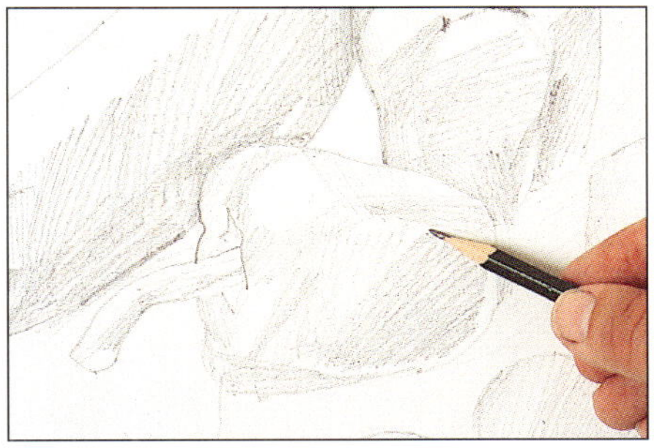

3 Check that everything is positioned correctly and make any adjustments. Scribble on a mid tone to indicate which part of the object is darkest and begin to give some hint of its overall colour. Simple, directional shading helps suggest the planes or surface direction of the objects.

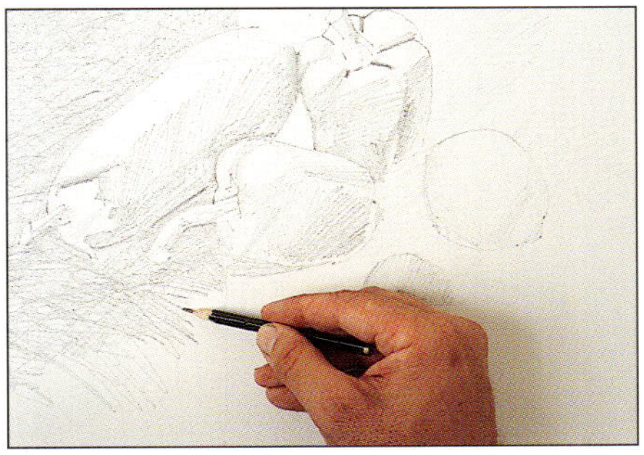

4 The tone representing the colour of the dark red sheet of paper begins to be built up with multi-directional scribbling. Work around the aubergine and pepper, allowing the scribbled tone to redefine their edge.

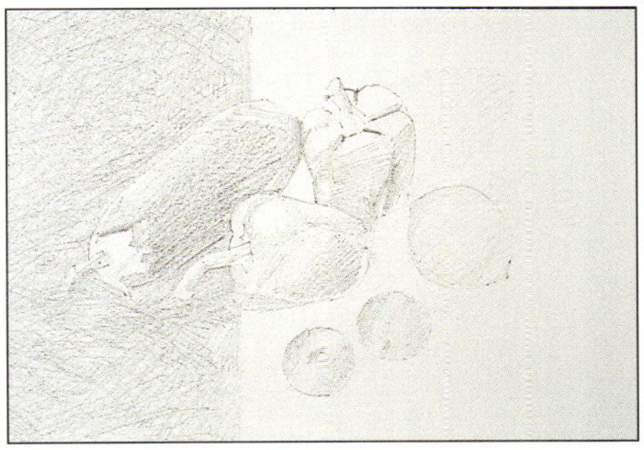

5 The drawing is now blocked in with tone so that the objects are beginning to appear three-dimensional, but the tones are all in the mid range. The tonal values need to be stretched and beefed up. Remember, it is always easier to darken a tone by working over it with pencil than it is to lighten one by using the eraser. To prevent the drawing from smudging as you work, and the side of your hand from becoming marked with graphite, rest your hand on a sheet of clean paper placed over the drawing.

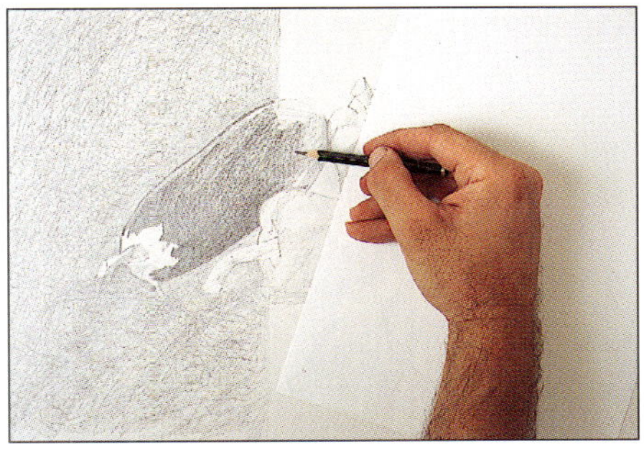

6 The dark, almost black, tone of the aubergine is scribbled in. All other tones will be made relative to this. Marks on the drawing board can sometimes show through when working hard and dark in this way, but you can avoid this by placing an extra sheet or two of paper beneath the sheet on which you are working

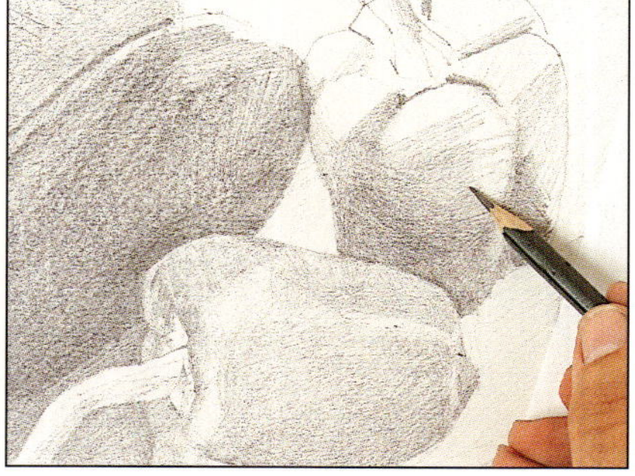

7 Work over the peppers, darkening and modifying the complex tones and balancing their depth and intensity against that of the aubergine. Notice how the shadow on the green pepper at the back is as dark in tone as the purple aubergine.

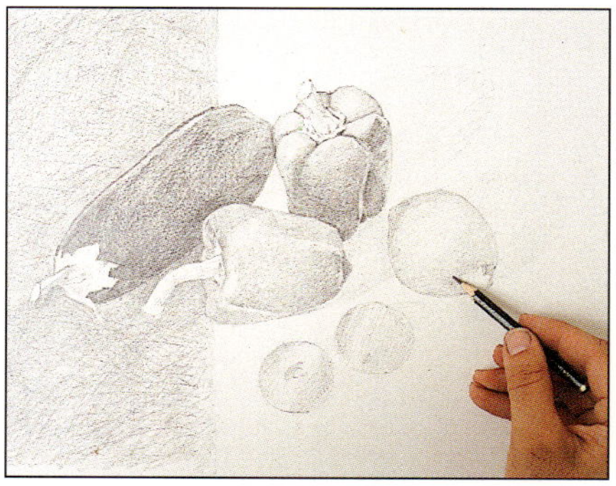

8 The lemon on the right is the lightest object in the group, but it is still considerably darker than the white surface on which it is sitting. The lines outlining the lemon are made to disappear by working the tone right up to them.

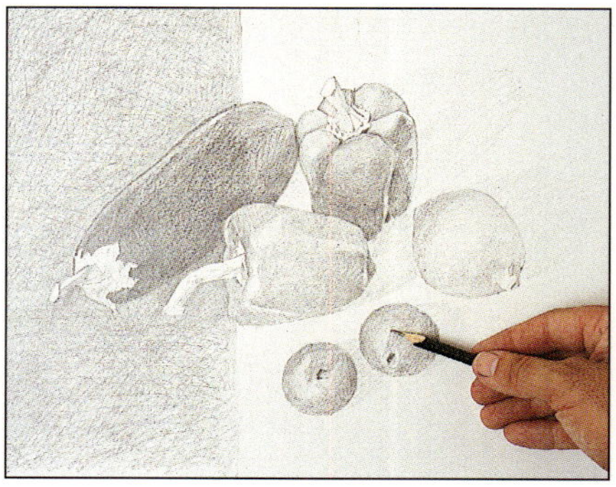

9 The plums are worked on next. Work the tone around the surface, allowing the white paper to show through in order to suggest the reflected highlight.

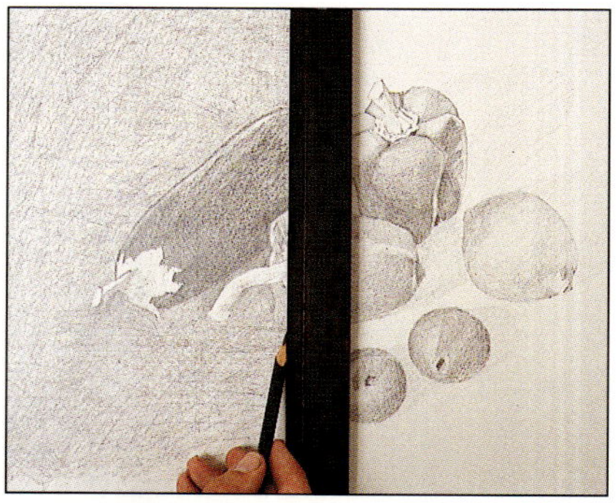

10 The dark red paper needs to be darker and the edge crisper. This is done by placing a ruler on the drawing so it can be used as a mask, and scribbling right up to it with the pencil.

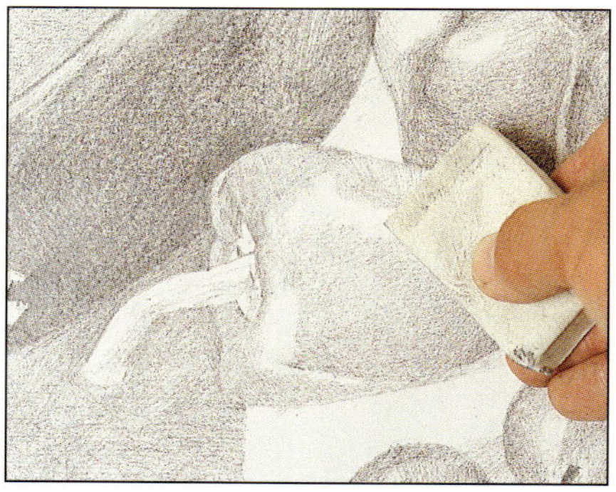

11 The highlights are lightened and the background around the shadows cleaned using the putty eraser.

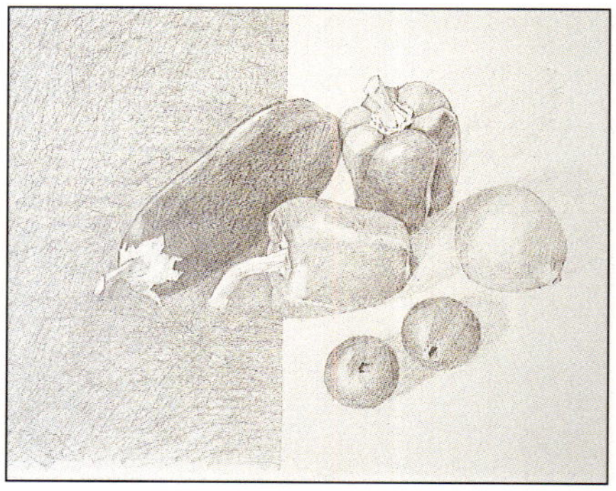

12 The scribbled shading successfully shows the form, mass and volume of the objects, hints at the differences in their colour, and also describes the smoothness of the aubergine and peppers and the subtle, pitted texture of the lemon. The dark sheet of paper placed behind the aubergine balances the large area of white on which the rest of the group is placed.

# Alternative Approaches

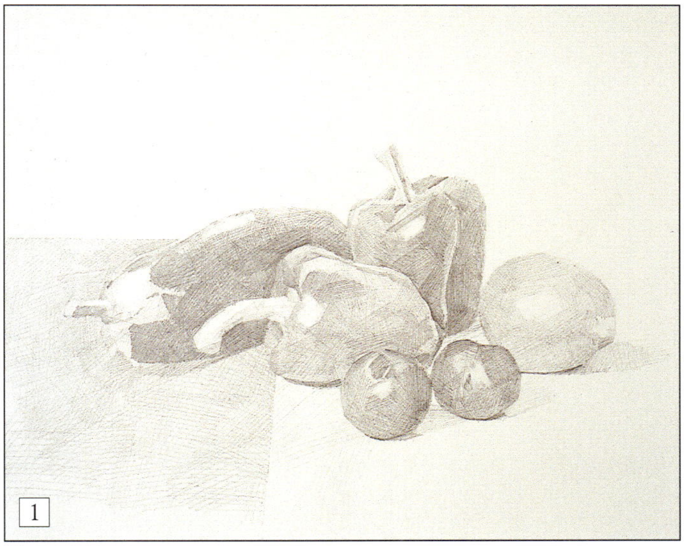

1 The viewpoint has been changed but the composition and the position of the group remain the same. Using controlled cross-hatching made with a single sharp HB pencil, the tones are gradually built up until their values work in relation to each another. The lightest areas are covered with almost imperceptible light hatching, while the darkest areas are layered with heavier, denser cross-hatching.

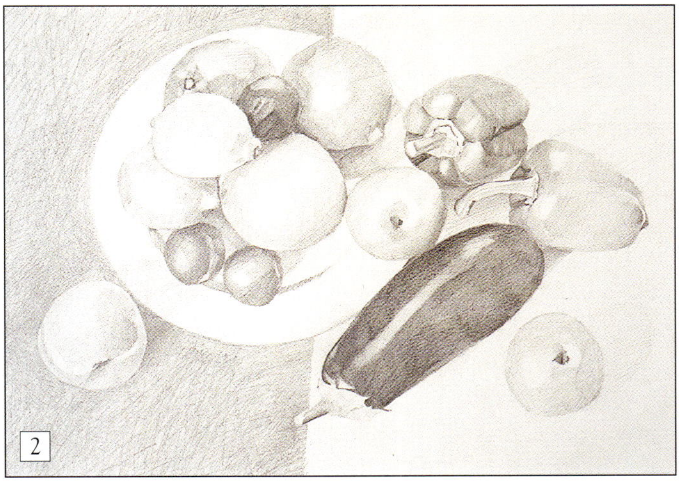

2 The still life is elaborated with more fruit, which is piled onto a white plate. The sheet of red paper is used again, but this time it is positioned so that it dissects the composition almost in half. Because the dark paper runs underneath the plate it defines the plate's white shape and throws it forward. The composition works because the dark mass of the paper is balanced by the dark of the aubergine and peppers on the right. The unusual viewpoint serves to give the drawing an almost abstract quality.

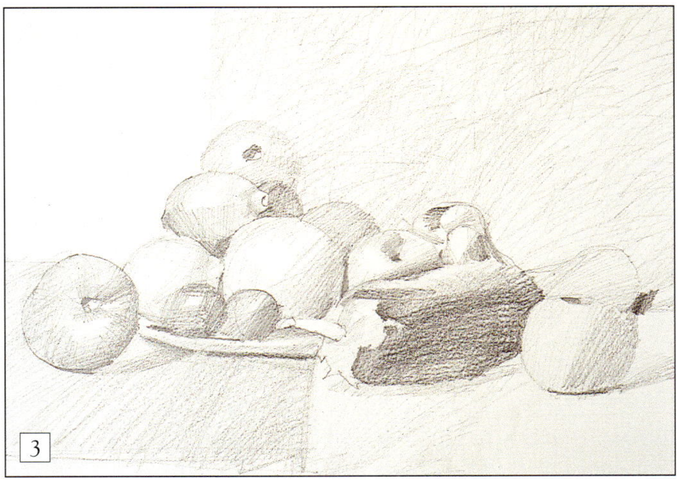

3 A composition similar to the above is given a much looser and faster treatment using a very soft 6B graphite stick. The forms, this time viewed from the side, are treated simply with scribbled tone helping them to read as round, solid objects. An area of tone has been added partway across the background, acting as a compositional device to add interest and balance to the top half of the drawing.

# MONT ST MICHEL

*Graphite*

PROJECT THREE

COMBINING A NUMBER OF different techniques in a single drawing opens up exciting possibilities. Drawings that are executed using one technique alone, while often being competent drawings, can look tired. These flat or weary-looking pictures can be perked up by introducing new or different marks, or by working over and into the drawing with a different medium, but the simplest answer is not to allow your drawings to become dull and jaded in the first place.

Some media are better suited than others for making a wide and varied range of marks. The humble pencil is one of these, as is its close but more versatile and flexible cousin the graphite stick. When used with graphite powder the graphite stick can produce stimulating, rich drawings containing a wealth of exciting marks and techniques.

Graphite is a quick medium. Its nature and characteristics seem to encourage the artist to work with some urgency, which, if working from the landscape, or *en plein air*, is no bad thing, given the often capricious nature of the weather. The landscape – and the weather, which has an immediate effect on it – are infinitely variable, providing the artist with an ideal opportunity to practise with the mark-making capabilities of a medium.

A well-chosen position from which to work can make the difference between a successful and a less successful drawing. Bear in mind that a very small shift in viewpoint can considerably alter the scene in front of you. When choosing a place to work, always try to look for the unusual.

Clever use of composition and the illusion of depth through the utilisation of atmospheric or aerial perspective are two important considerations. Composition is about visually balancing all the elements within your picture. Colour, space, scale, form and texture all play a part and can be used to compose and structure your drawing.

Various formulae exist for composition, based on precise mathematical calculations that divide the picture area up into an ideal, underlying grid on which to work. Perhaps the best known of these is the golden section. A simple yet alternative method of balancing your drawing is to divide the picture area approximately into thirds. First draw a rectangle on a sheet of paper, then divide the rectangle horizontally and vertically into thirds by drawing lines across the rectangle to mark the position of the divisions. This will give you a basic grid. The theory is that by positioning important elements or focal points on or about these dividing lines, or at the four points where the lines intersect each other, gives a satisfying arrangement.

The rule works, but rules, as we know, are made to be broken. A useful aid to composition can be made by taking a smallish rectangular sheet of card and cutting a slightly smaller rectangle from the centre. Stretch four elastic bands over the card, two across the horizontal and two across the vertical, thus dividing the rectangular hole you cut into thirds. The grid that is formed can be held up as a viewfinder, and will assist you in making decisions on composition and format.

## MATERIALS AND EQUIPMENT

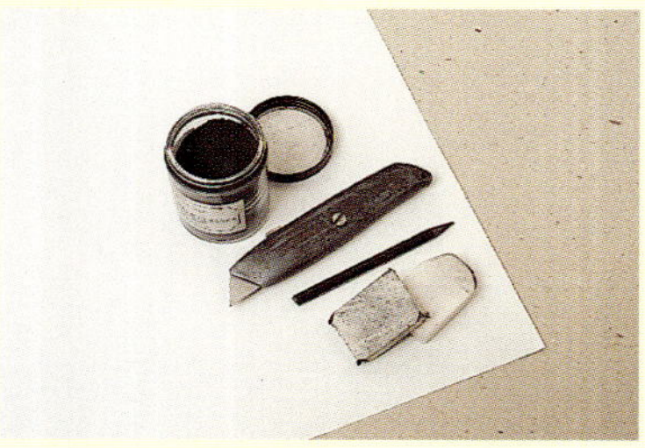

- Sheet of medium-weight A2 paper
- Graphite powder
- Stanley knife or craft knife
- 4B pencil
- Putty eraser, plastic or rubber eraser

The use of aerial perspective helps solve the problems that can occur when trying to give depth to a drawing. As a rule, because of the effects of atmosphere, tone and colour will become lighter the further away they are from the onlooker. Distant objects also appear smaller and less well defined than those which are close to; close objects therefore appear to be in sharper focus, darker in colour and tone and larger. The view of Mont St Michel in Brittany illustrates these two principles of composition and perspective. The subject is a simple one, with – on first sight– little with which to work.

For your drawing, use an A2 sheet of medium-weight cartridge paper with a 4B graphite stick and graphite powder. Various erasers are needed to draw into the powder, and fixative to prevent smudging,

# The Drawing

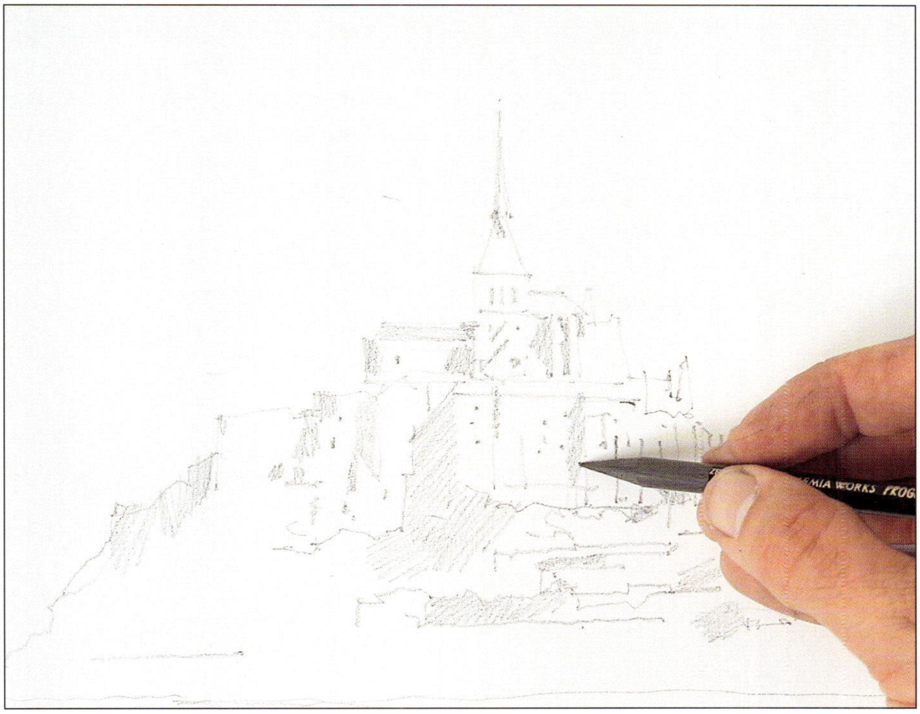

1 Using the 4B graphite pencil the subject is positioned on the sheet of paper about a third of the way in from the right-hand side, and just below the halfway point from the bottom. The buildings are drawn in lightly: being in the distance they are indistinct and pale in tone. The graphite pencil can make a dense black, so work carefully, with just enough pressure to make a mark. This will be easier if you hold the pencil loosely and not too near the point.

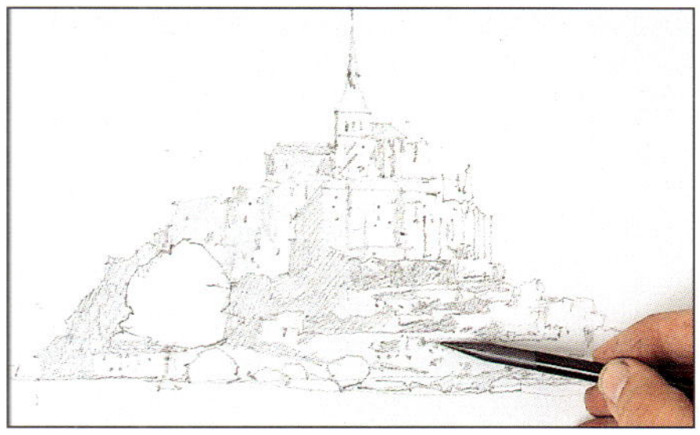

2 The buildings and trees on the mount are elaborated. A few windows and other details are indicated. Below, but in front of the mount in the middle distance, the row of trees and bushes running off to the left-hand side of the drawing are sketched in.

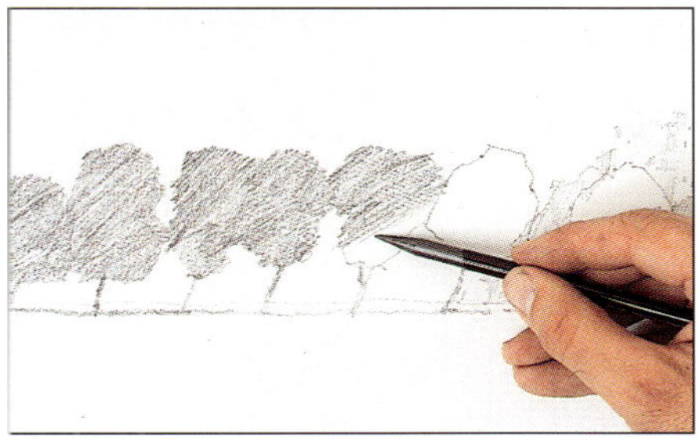

3 The foliage on the trees is loosely scribbled in. As your draw, turn the pencil between the fingers to retain the point. The trees must be darker than the buildings and the mount in the distance. This makes them appear to sit in front of the distant abbey, occupying their correct position in the middle distance.

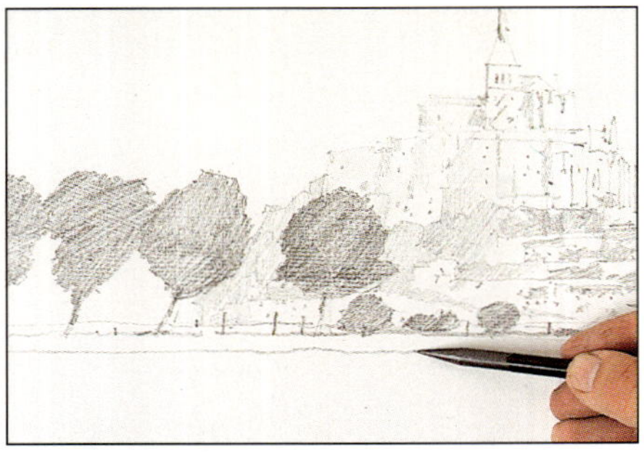

4 The bank of grass below the trees is drawn next and blocked in with scribbled tone. Broken fence posts and a few bushes are indicated.

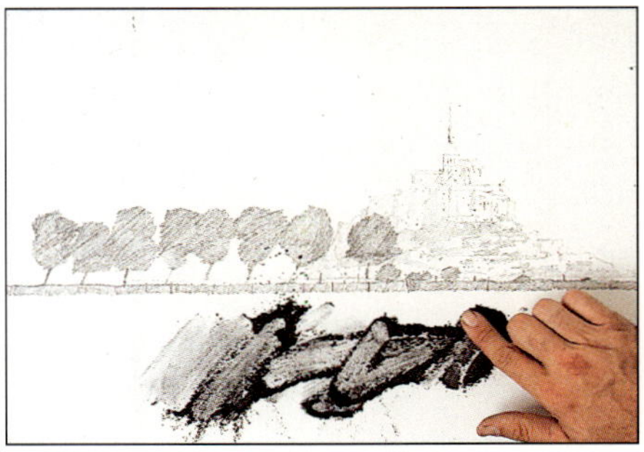

5 With the drawing lying flat, a little graphite powder is tipped onto the lower part of the drawing. Be careful not to pour out too much: you may find it easier to control if you remove powder from the jar with a spoon or palette knife. Spread the powder out across the area to be covered by using a finger, or, if you prefer, a piece of tissue or torchon. Any excess powder can be poured back into the jar.

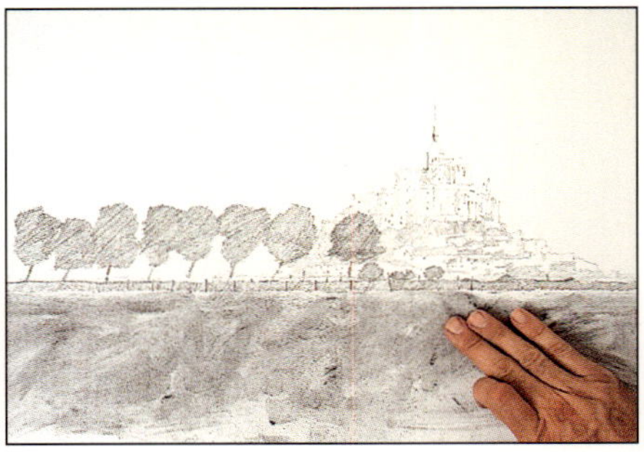

6 Make sure your hands and fingers are dry, and without pressing too hard, rub the powder into the paper. Don't worry if the result looks a little uneven.

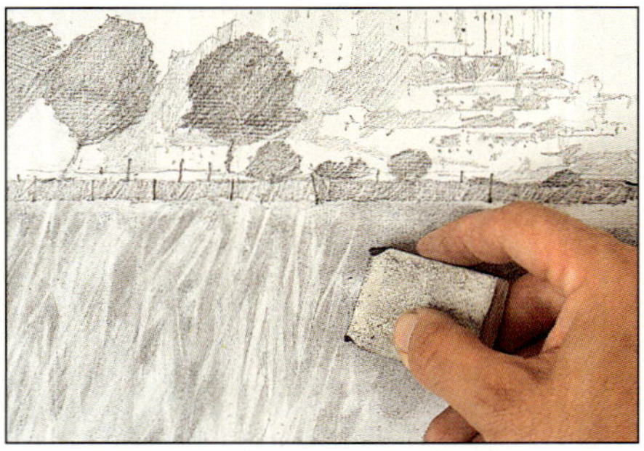

7 With the putty eraser, work into the powder, pulling it off in lines to represent an overgrown field of grass or a crop of cereal. The eraser will get dirty very quickly and will then start to smear the graphite rather than remove it. Cut off a slice of the eraser with a sharp knife to get a new clean edge.

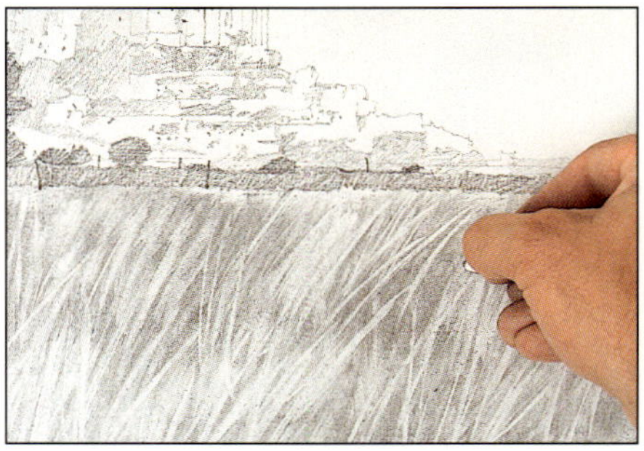

8 Finer, thinner marks can be made by slicing a harder plastic or rubber eraser at a sharp angle. Again, once the eraser is covered with graphite it will cease to work and will need recutting.

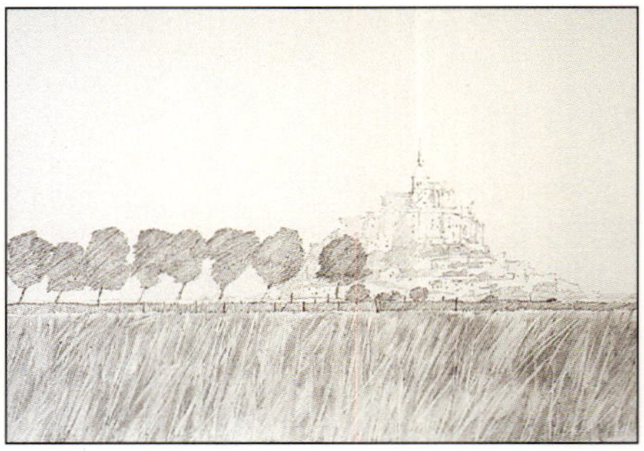

9 The finished drawing is a balanced composition, alive with a variety of marks. The foreground could easily be worked into further with soft graphite sticks or, once the drawing as been fixed, worked over with more powder. As it was a clear day the sky has been left as white paper, but powder could be used there too, gradually lightening it as the horizon or distance is approached. An alternative is to work with the eraser, cutting out dramatic cloud formations.

# Alternative Approaches

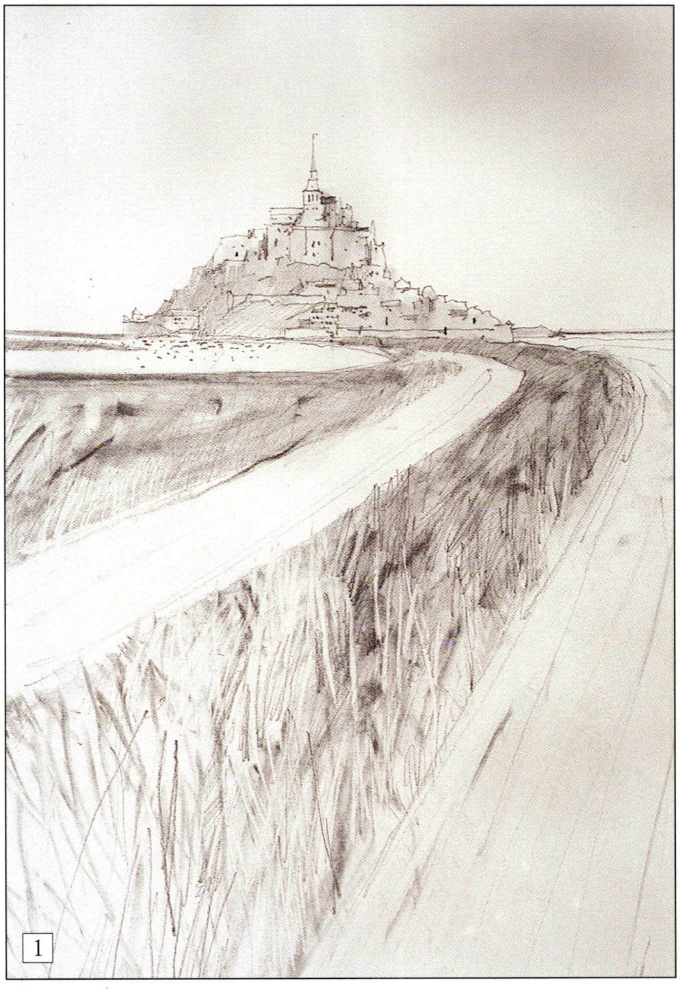


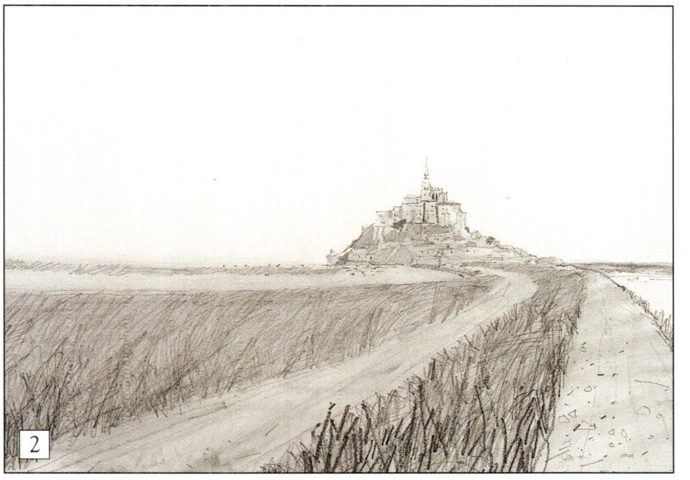


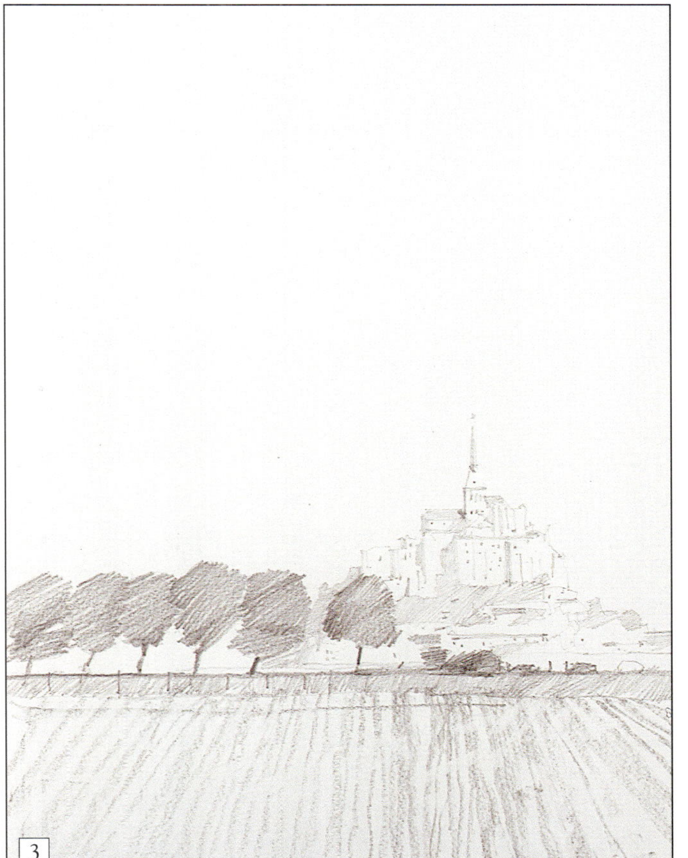


**1** Switching format can help composition too. In this drawing a portrait (vertical) format is used to make more of the flat foreground and the curving road. The centre of interest, the abbey, sits about a third of the way down from the top of the drawing, and just short of halfway in from the left. The eye is drawn up to the abbey by the road curving towards it.

**2** Breaking rules when drawing and painting is all part of the fun. Here the line of the horizon runs straight across the middle of the drawing. The mount sits on the horizon just off centre.jutting up into the sky. Balance is achieved with tone and texture. The foreground is heavily worked, while the sky is plain white paper. The on-looker's eye is taken to the lower half of the drawing by the depth of tone and the texture, but then, again, is immediately taken back to the abbey by the road curving towards it.

**3** Here a vast expanse of featureless sky balances the buildings, trees and field at the bottom. The abbey spire lures the eye up to the heavens, but it falls back to earth, pulled by the interest below. Again, the attention is focused on the row of trees and the abbey, all sitting on a line a third of the way up the drawing.

# A YOUNG GIRL

*Charcoal*

PROJECT FOUR

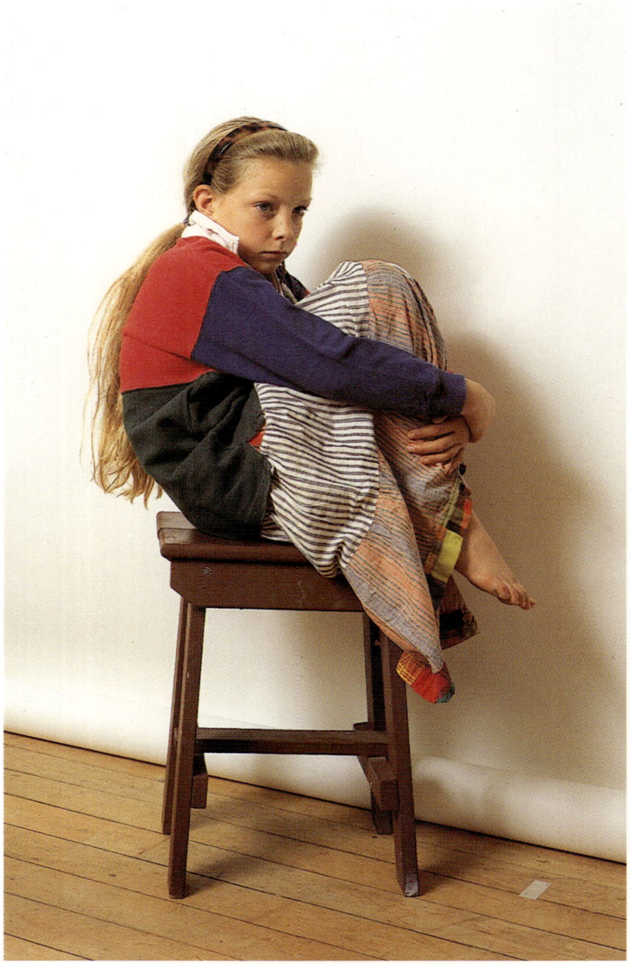

WHILE IT IS PERFECTLY possible to work at any scale with any medium, and in any style, with certain media more than others there does seem to be an optimum size. Charcoal is a case in point. At best, working small can be difficult, and you will find yourself unable to use to the full the many qualities and characteristics of the media.

Charcoal has long been favoured as a medium for teaching drawing, as its very nature forces a broader approach that precludes becoming too involved in details. Laying down tone in charcoal is fast and easy, and it is happily married with a host of other media. However, the real beauty of charcoal comes from its ability to create a dark, sensual line that is quick to produce, one that can easily be varied in thickness and intensity. Any unfixed marks can simply be dusted off, making corrections and erasing an easy matter.

Charcoal will smudge if brushed against, so drawing should be done with the hand kept free of the paper surface, and only the charcoal coming into contact with it. This gives looser, flowing strokes that result from using the whole arm rather than just the wrist. Lines in the wrong place or of the wrong thickness are inevitable. A flick of a soft rag and all that is left is a ghost of an image, which remains as a useful guide for making your correction.

Work with a sheet of paper secured to a drawing board held vertically on an easel or propped against a chair. Standing makes moving easier and so the marks made with the charcoal will appear less restrained and more fluid.

This project demonstrates that matching the subject to the medium can pay dividends. The girl was dressed specifically for the type of drawings that were planned: the shirt and dress are full of linear patterns that give a clue to the form beneath; this, together with long hair falling down her back, presents a perfect subject for the graceful, confident lines that can be made with a stick of charcoal. A thick and a thin stick of medium charcoal were used on a sheet of 140lb Not surface watercolour paper.

## MATERIALS AND EQUIPMENT

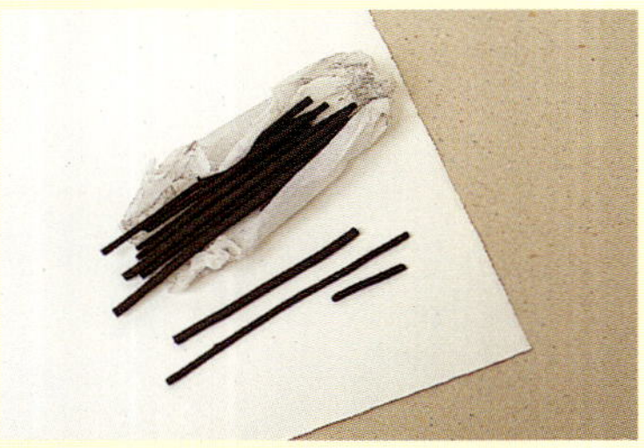

- 28x21 in sheet of 140lb Not watercolour paper
- Medium sticks of charcoal, thick and thin

# The Drawing

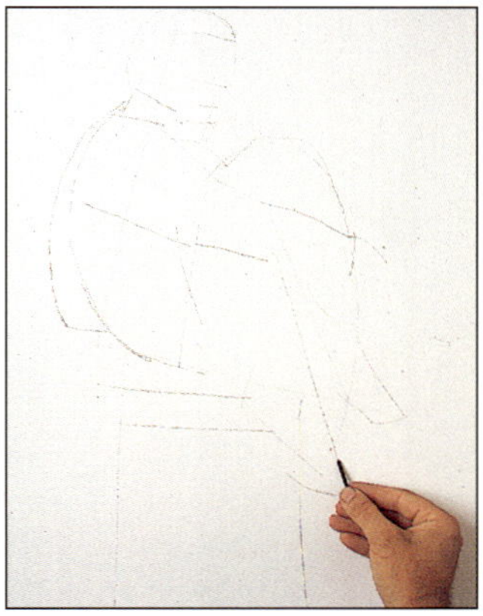

1 A few preliminary measurements were made and the overall shapes of the figure and stool sketched in lightly. The shapes suggest a triangle sitting on an upright rectangle. Draw in the approximate directions of the arm, the fall of the hair and the curve of the head. Hold the charcoal high up to encourage a light line.

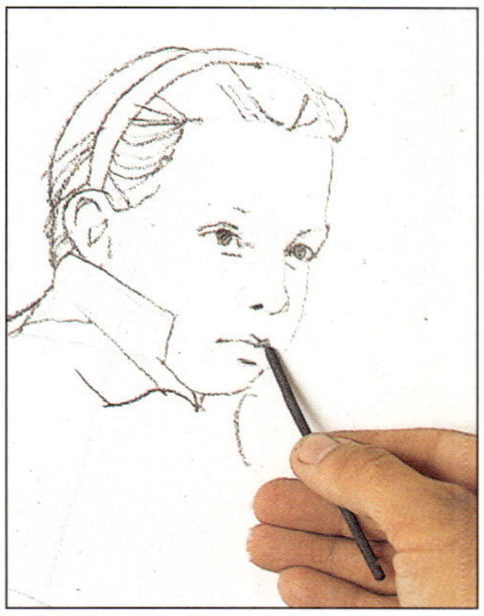

2 Working without too much pressure, draw in the shape of the head and the features. Pay particular attention to the angle of the eyes, nose and mouth relative to the angle of the head.

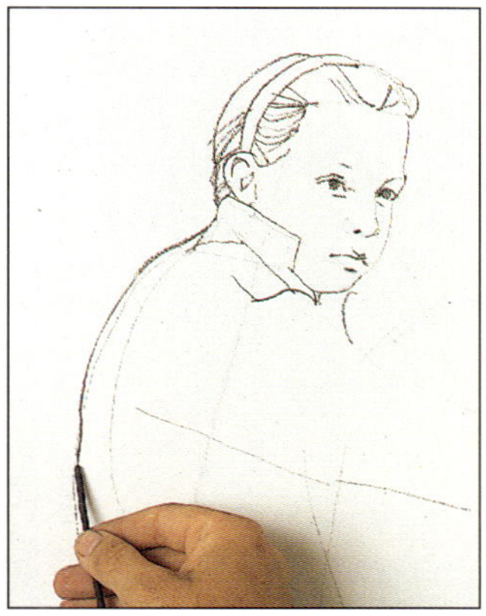

3 Working in fluid lines of varying thickness, sketch in the hair using the light construction lines as a guide.

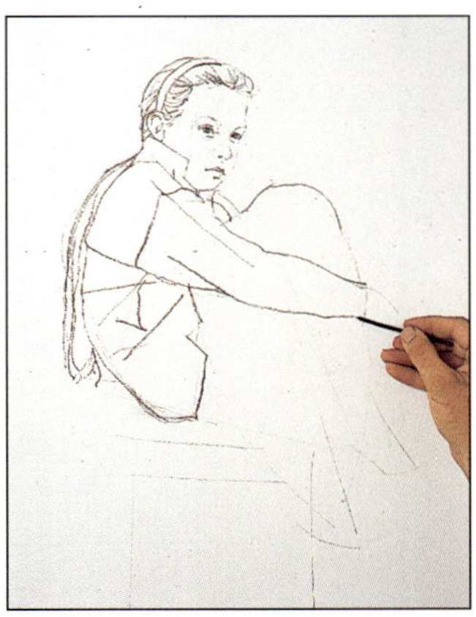

4 Work around the torso, describing the contours of the shirt. Use the seams, the change in pattern and the lines created by the folds of the cloth to help describe the form. Describe the arc of the dress lying taut across the knees, and the upper and lower edge of the sleeve. Indicate the fall of the skirt down the front of the leg.

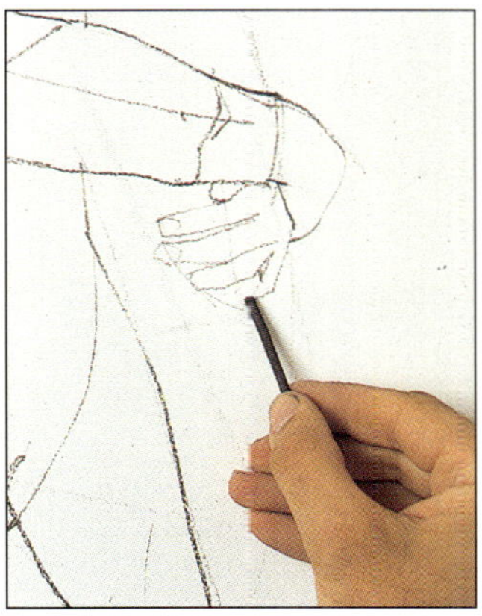

5 The fingers of the hand are drawn lightly, curving around and holding on to the leg. Try to vary the line thickness to give a suggestion of light and shade. Notice how the line describing the uppermost hand is thicker and darker where it rests across the other hand.

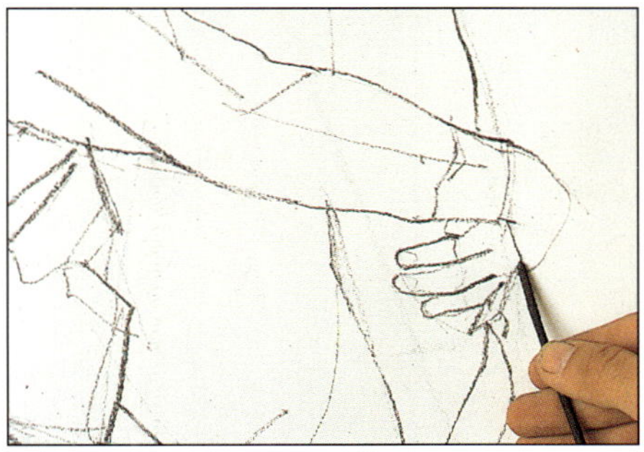

6 Once the hand is drawn correctly in light charcoal it can be redrawn using more pressure to produce a darker line.

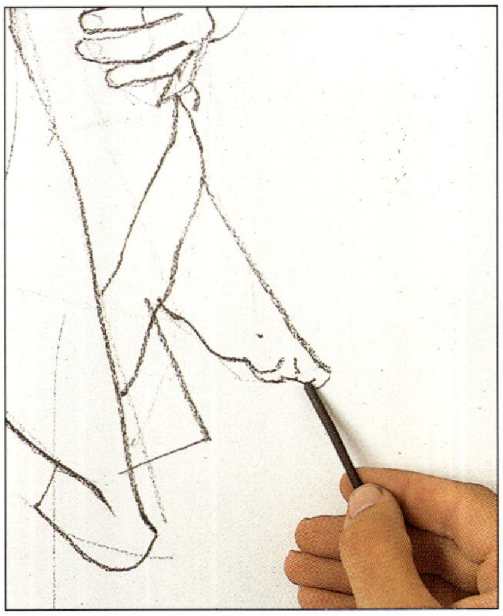

7 Feet are notoriously difficult to draw convincingly; the simpler the treatment the better. Try describing them with as few lines as possible. Here the top of the foot is almost straight with a slight bump at the end. The bottom of the foot curls around into the little toe. The position of the other toes are merely hinted at.

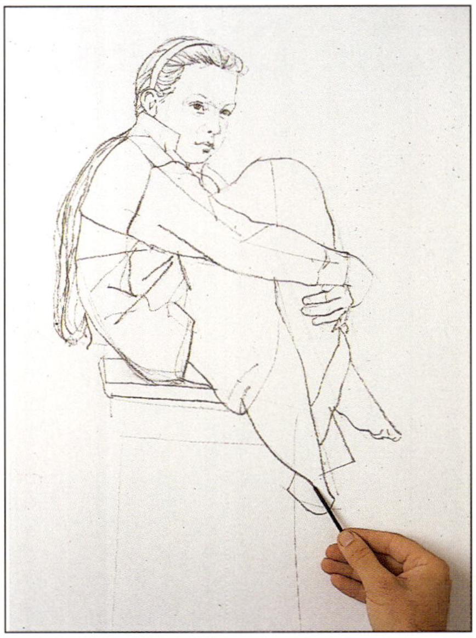

8 Draw in the seat of the chair and finish the flowing line of the dress. Indicating the line of a few creases helps the dress to hang from the body.

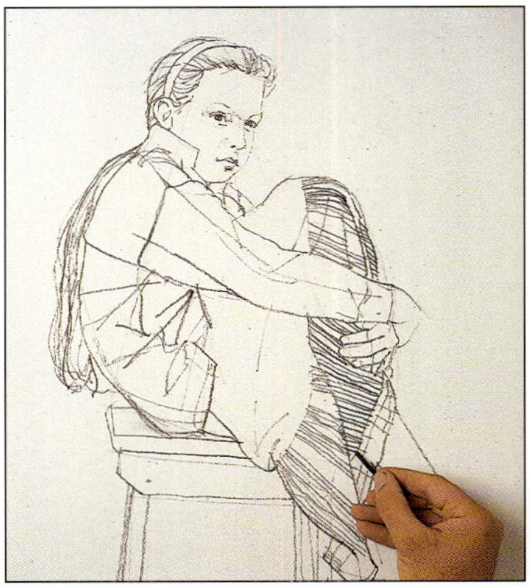

9 The legs of the chair are drawn and the hair falling down the child's back is reworked, drawing a few long, light lines. Lines of shadow and folds of material are redefined on the shirt, and the lines of the pattern are stroked in on the skirt using more pressure to make a darker mark.

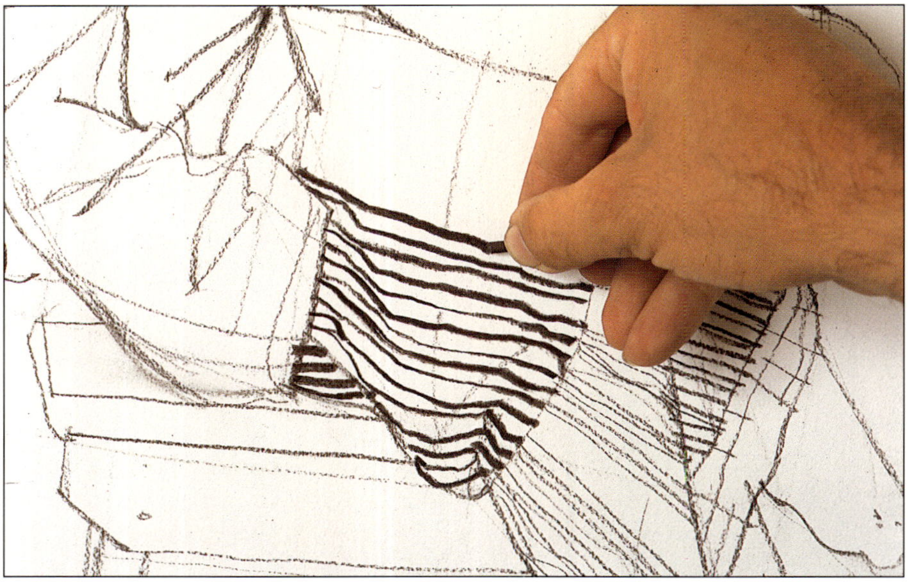

10 With a thicker piece of charcoal held close to the end, draw the rest of the pattern lines, following and using the contours and folds of the dress as a guide. Draw with a dark line; if the pressure shatters the stick of charcoal, simply break the end square and carry on.

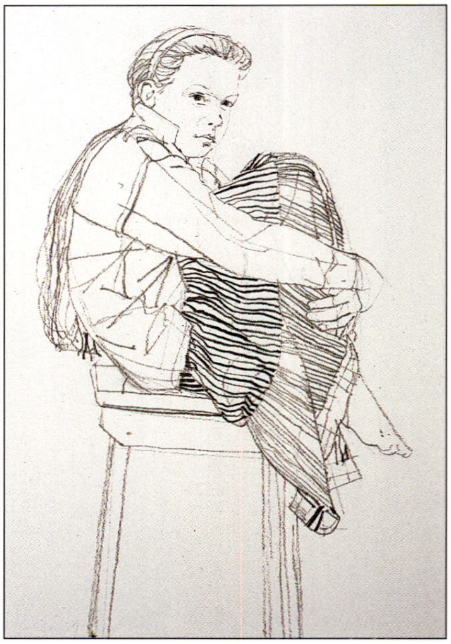

11 Complete the pattern on the dress and make adjustments to the hair and skirt folds. The finished drawing shows how variety in the quality of line can successfully describe pattern, direction, light and shade, and thus form.

# Alternative Approaches

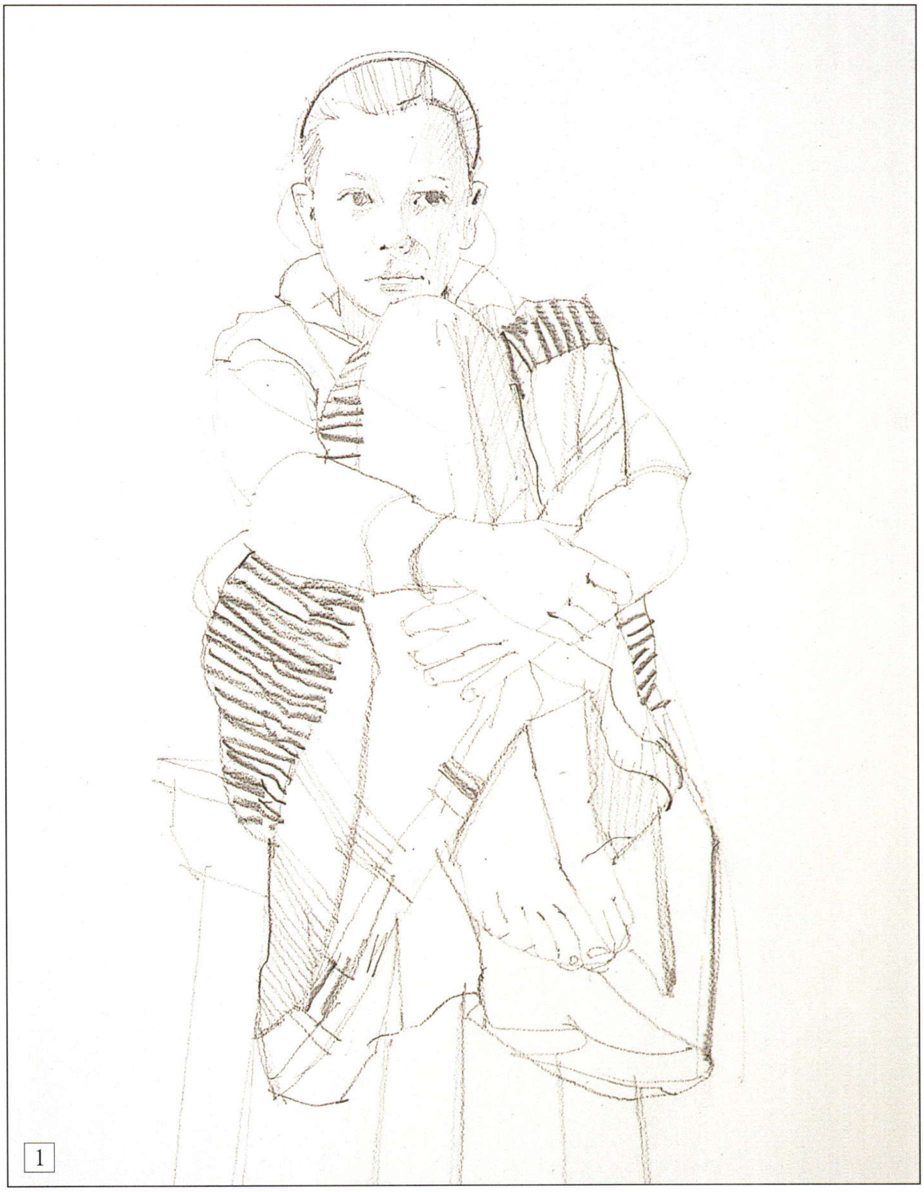

1

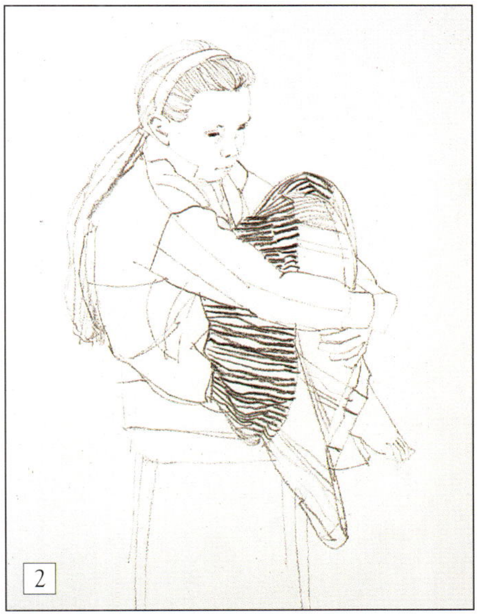

2

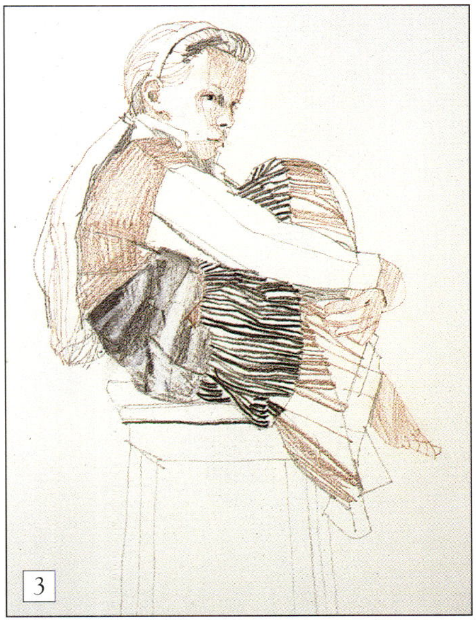

3

**1** This drawing has been done with a sharpened stick of black conté. The quality of the line is lighter and more subtle than the charcoal. Conté sticks can be difficult to erase so by working lightly mistakes can simply be corrected and redrawn and will not be too glaringly obvious in the finished work. Once the drawing looks right it can be redrawn using a darker line. The pattern on the skirt was drawn using the blunt square end of the stick.

**2** Changing the viewpoint gives the drawing a little more depth. This is because the top of the head, the curve of the shoulder, the skirt stretched over the knees, the top of the foot and the seat of the stool are all visible. These planes or perspectives take us into the drawing.

**3** Mixing media is always fun and the results sometimes surprising. Here the figure has been drawn with a mixture of black and sanguine conté, charcoal and white chalk. The sanguine was used for the skin and the hair, and gave colour to the shirt and the pattern on the skirt. The heavy dark of the charcoal completes the pattern and the bottom of the shirt.

# HAT, COAT AND BAG

*Charcoal and White Chalk*

PROJECT FIVE

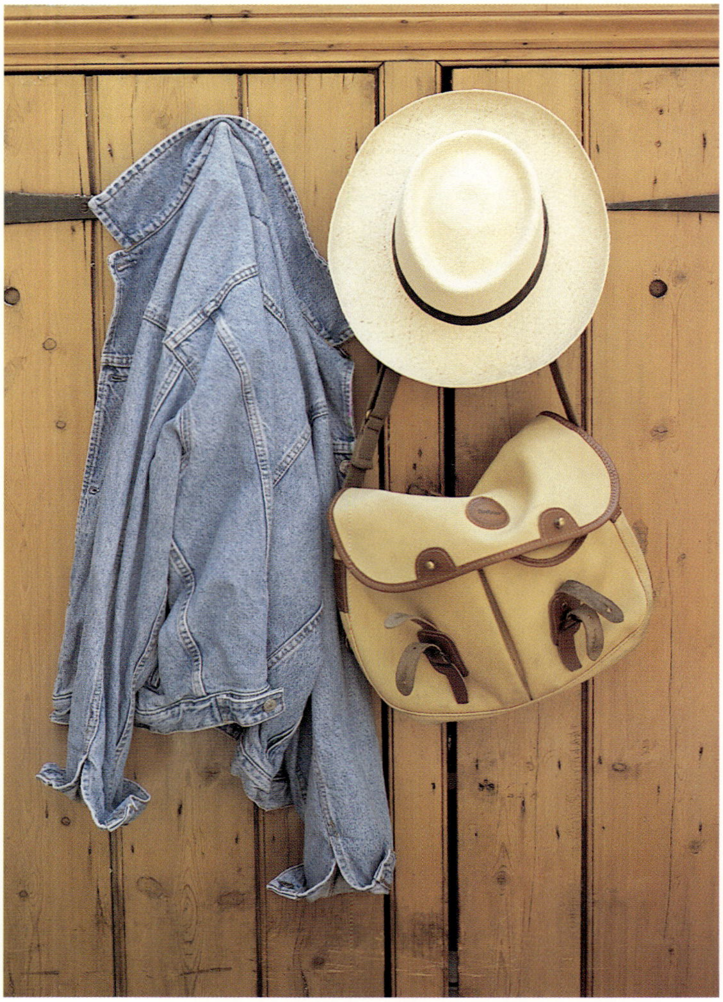

THE QUALITIES that are to be found in many monochromatic (single colour) drawings can be extended further by working on toned or tinted paper. Charcoal, because of its density and strength, is the perfect medium for this traditional technique, because when working tonally on a white ground it can be difficult to judge the strength of the tones against the white of the support. Draw a line of charcoal on a sheet of white paper and another line – using equal pressure – on a sheet of tinted paper, and you will notice how much darker the mark reads on the white sheet.

Another traditional way of working is to establish the mid tones first, then judge the density of the lights and darks against them. By choosing a mid-tone paper the charcoal is used to give the mid to dark tones and white chalk or conté is used to pull out the lighter tones. The paper will show through your drawing, giving an overall sense of harmony. You can work on paper of any colour, but a more satisfactory result will be achieved if the tones and colours used are chosen from the many neutral greys, browns and ochres available from the various manufacturers.

Deciding what to draw is often a real problem for the beginner, yet the fact is, everything can be seen as a subject. However what inspires and excites one person to reach for their drawing materials will do nothing for another.

Suitable subjects are all around and we don't need to look far to find one. Here a straw hat, denim jacket and canvas bag made ideal subjects for a few hours' drawing. The drawing was made on a sheet of Ingres paper using thin willow charcoal, a thick stick of charcoal, white conté, a torchon and a putty eraser.

## Materials and Equipment

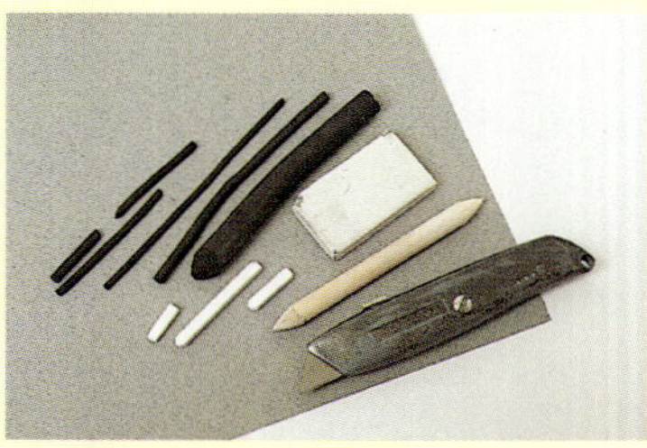

- 25x20 in sheet of mid-grey Ingres paper
- Sticks of charcoal, one thin willow charcoal stick and one stick of thick charcoal
- Two sticks of white conté grades HB and 2B
- Torchon
- Putty eraser

# The Drawing

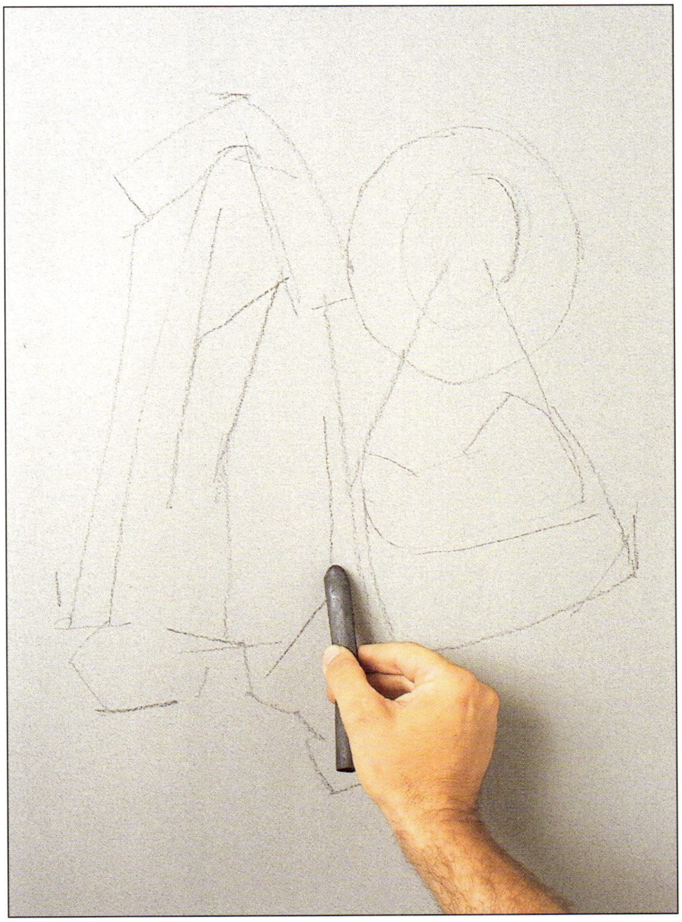

1 Position the hat, coat and bag centrally on the paper. Work lightly with as few strokes as possible, keeping the shapes basic. Pay particular attention to the angles of the jacket collar and the slant of the bag. If you do make a mistake, then simply reposition and redraw the line.

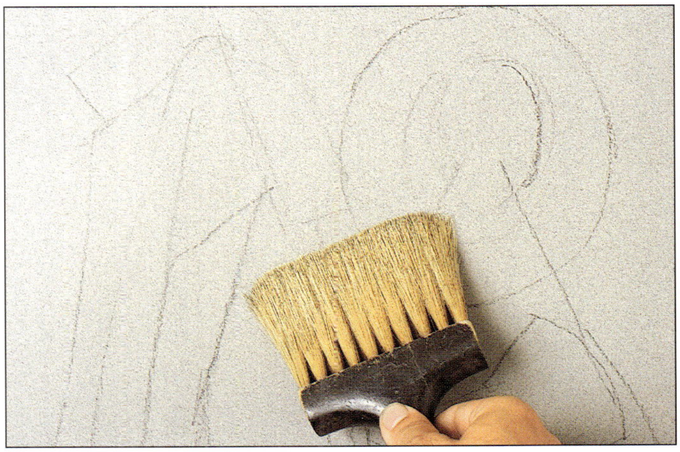

2 If the lines are a little dark lighten them by brushing over the drawing with a soft brush or by flicking a soft rag over the surface. Leave just the ghost of an image to act as a guide.

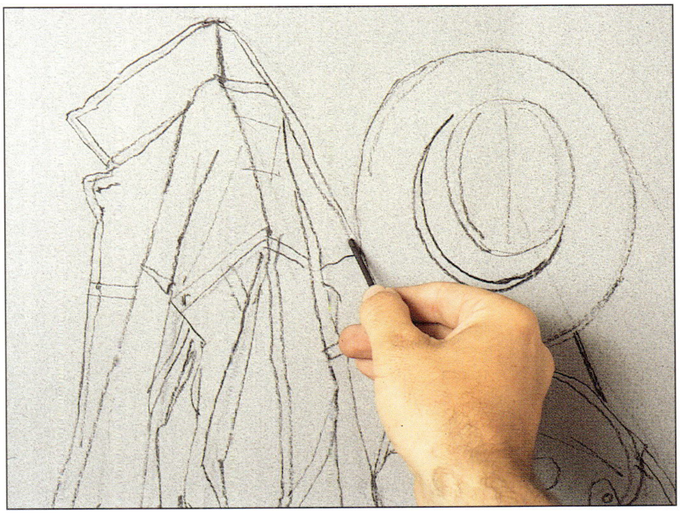

3 Once the subject has been positioned correctly you can begin to redraw with a thin stick of charcoal. Using the light drawing beneath as a guide, search out the folds and contours of the coat and bag. Pay particular attention to the oval shape of the hat and try to give the coat weight, so that it looks as if it is really hanging from a hook. The same applies to the bag; the dent in the top of the flap seems to suggest the bag has some weight. Once the drawing seems correct in line, it can be given a coat of fixative to prevent accidental smudges.

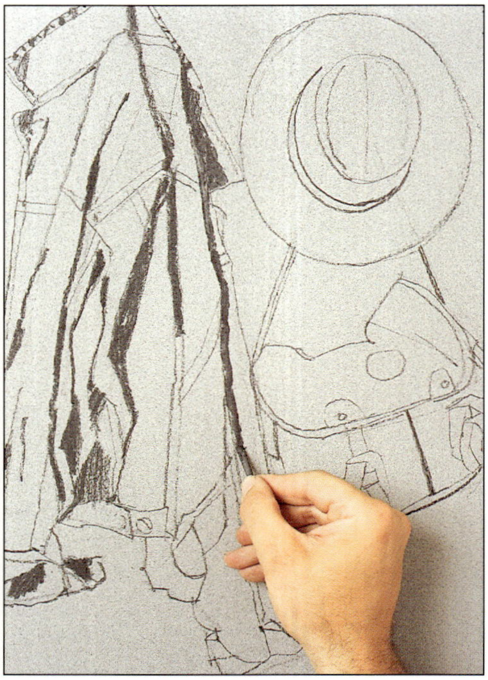

4 With a thin stick of charcoal, loosely and boldly lay in the dark shadows that are found in the creases of the jacket.

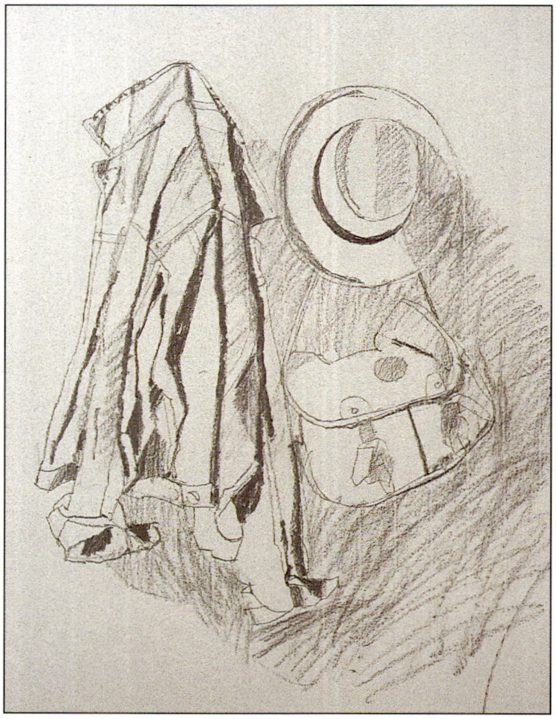

5 The dark of the hat band is laid on in the same way, and a dark definite shadow indicates the edge of the bag flap. The thicker stick of charcoal is then used to scribble loosely over the darker areas of the coat, the wall, the hat and around the buckles of the bag.

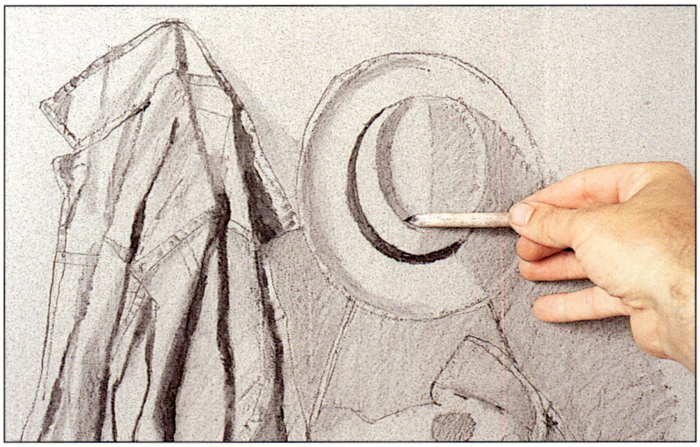

6 With the torchon, work over the drawing, blending and softening the dark charcoal. Pull and push tone over the paper surface. Pick up the charcoal dust on the torchon and use it to describe the detail in the seams of the jacket. Soften the shadows on the hat and smooth out the charcoal scribble on the wall.

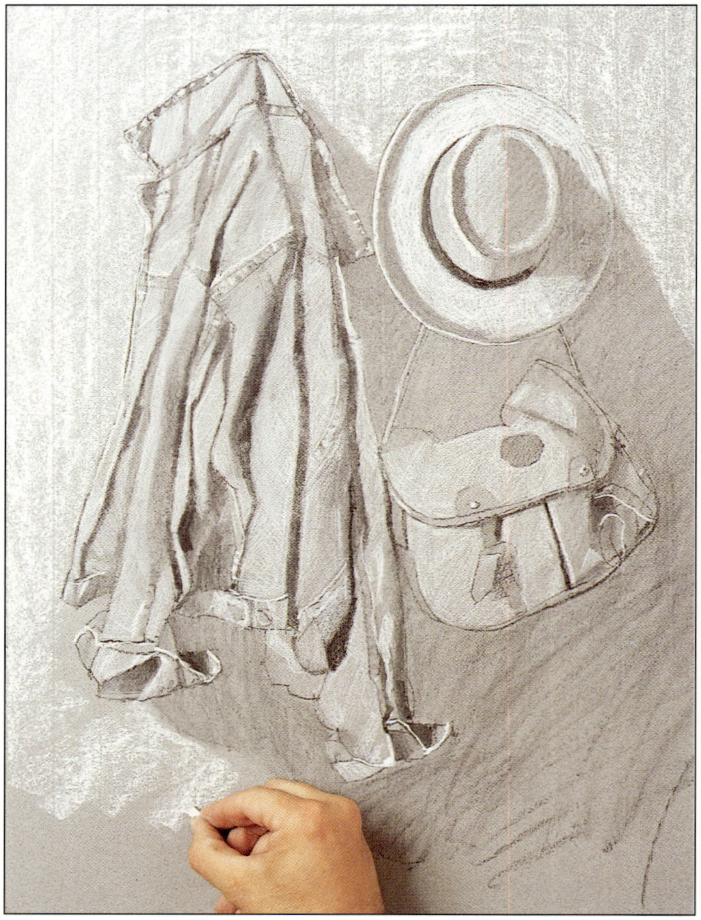

7 The putty eraser is used to cut back into the charcoal, making corrections, lightening tone and redrawing the way the folds in the cloth fall.

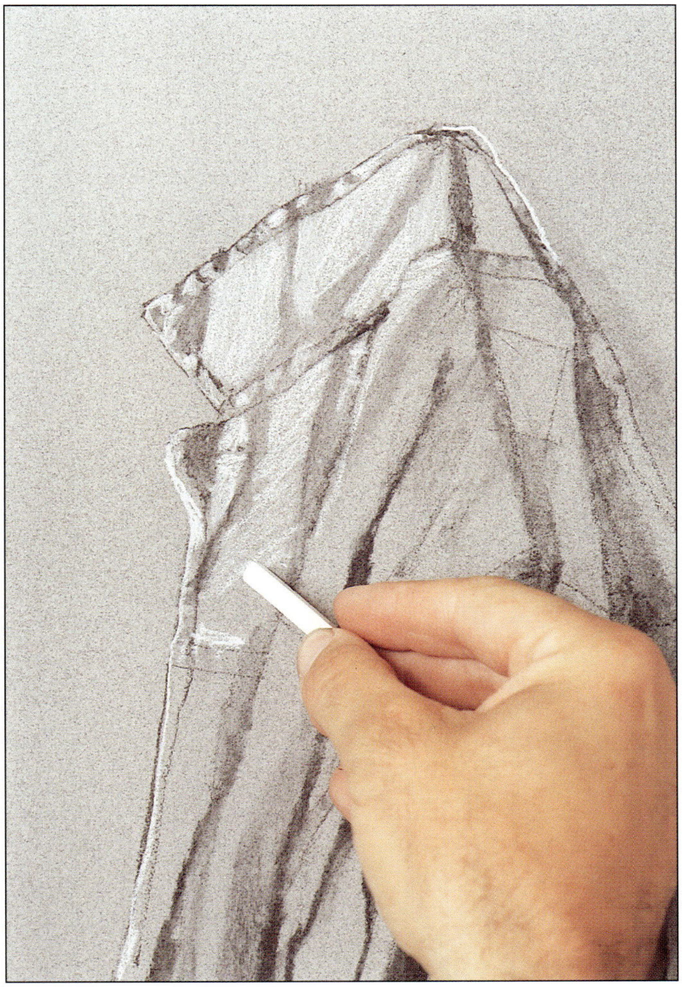

8 With the HB stick of conté chalk hatch in the lighter tones on the jacket. Work around the darker tones, moulding the material into folds and creases by highlighting with the chalk. Keep the hatching loose but controlled. The tight but visible lines of the hatching contrast with the softer blended areas of charcoal. They also suggest the weave of the material. Turn the chalk to get a sharp edge and run crisp light lines around the seams.

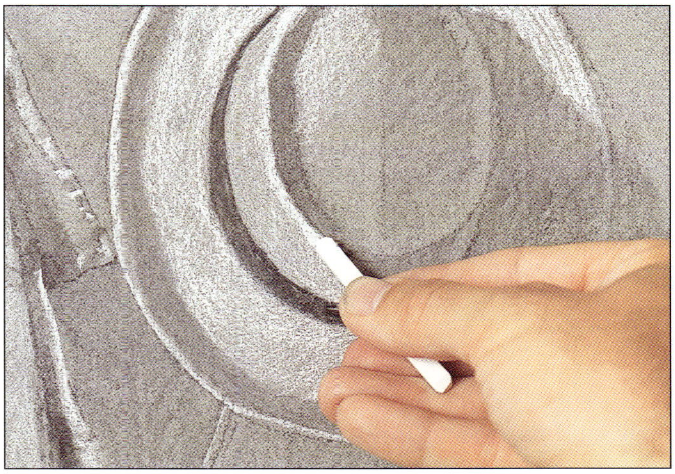

9 Move on to the hat. Lay in a flat, light, uniform tone around the brim and on the side towards the light. Holding the chalk close to the end press hard and draw a crisp line around the edge of the brim and around the top. Run a few light lines of chalk around the brim to suggest the weave of the straw.

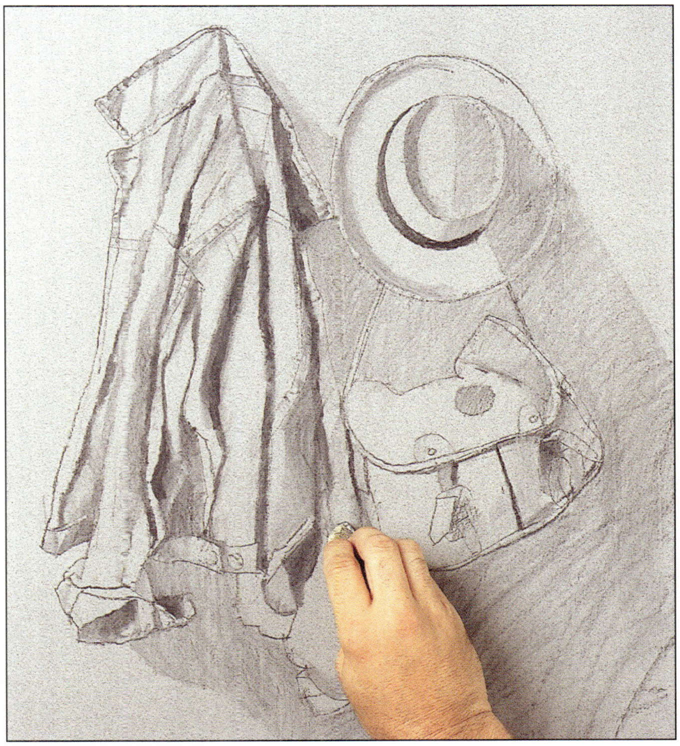

10 Light areas of tone are cross-hatched onto the top and front of the bag and crisp lines are drawn where the light catches the straps. Changing to the softer 2B crayon the background is laid in using the stick on its side to give a broad, flat stroke. Work carefully around the hat and jacket and cut in to define the shape of the shadow.

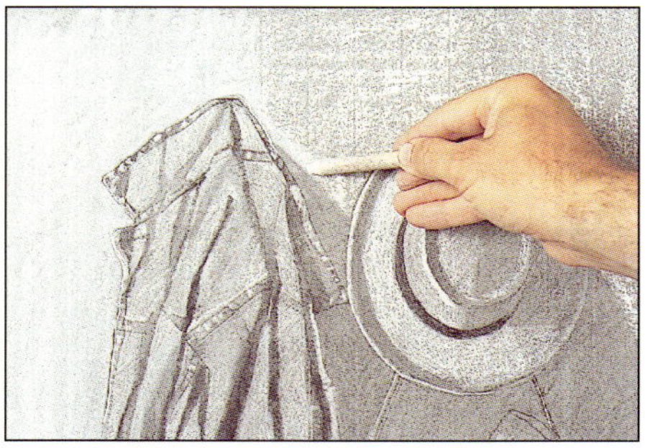

11 The torchon is used to blend the white chalk to give a uniform light tone across the background. For the flat open areas use your fingers or a clean rag. The edges of the jacket and hat are made sharper by working the chalk up close to make a clean line.

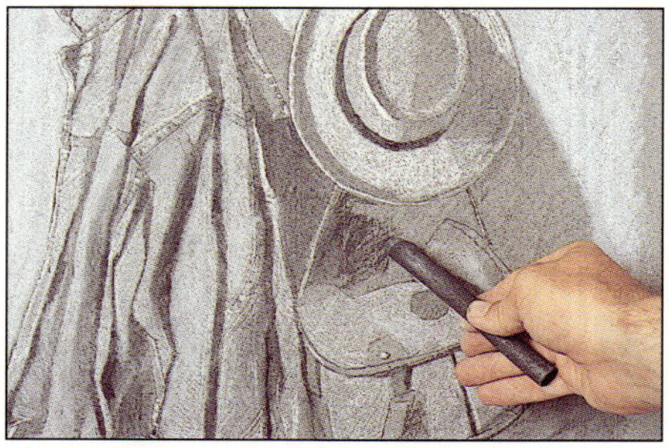

12 The drawing works tonally but looks a little flat, and could benefit from increasing the contrast between the lights and darks. The thick charcoal stick is used to darken in and around a few of the deeper folds on the jacket, and in the darkest area of shadow between the hat, coat and bag.

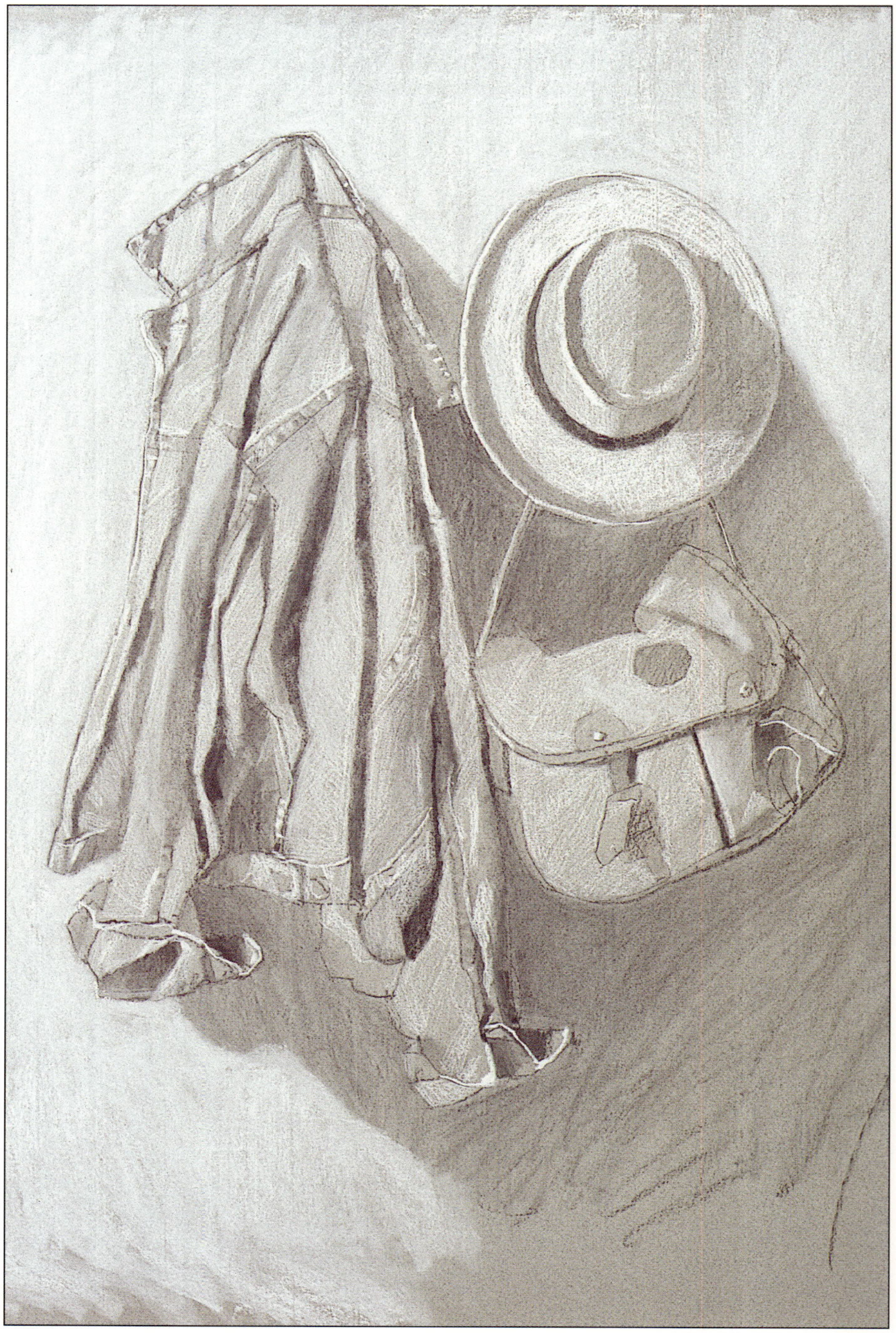

13 The finished drawing shows how the charcoal, chalk and tinted paper work together, creating a wide range of tones that describe the forms, creating depth in the shadows and height on the top of the hat. The shadow anchors the subjects to the wall while the light hatching and the sharp white lines jump forward toward the viewer.

# Alternative Approaches

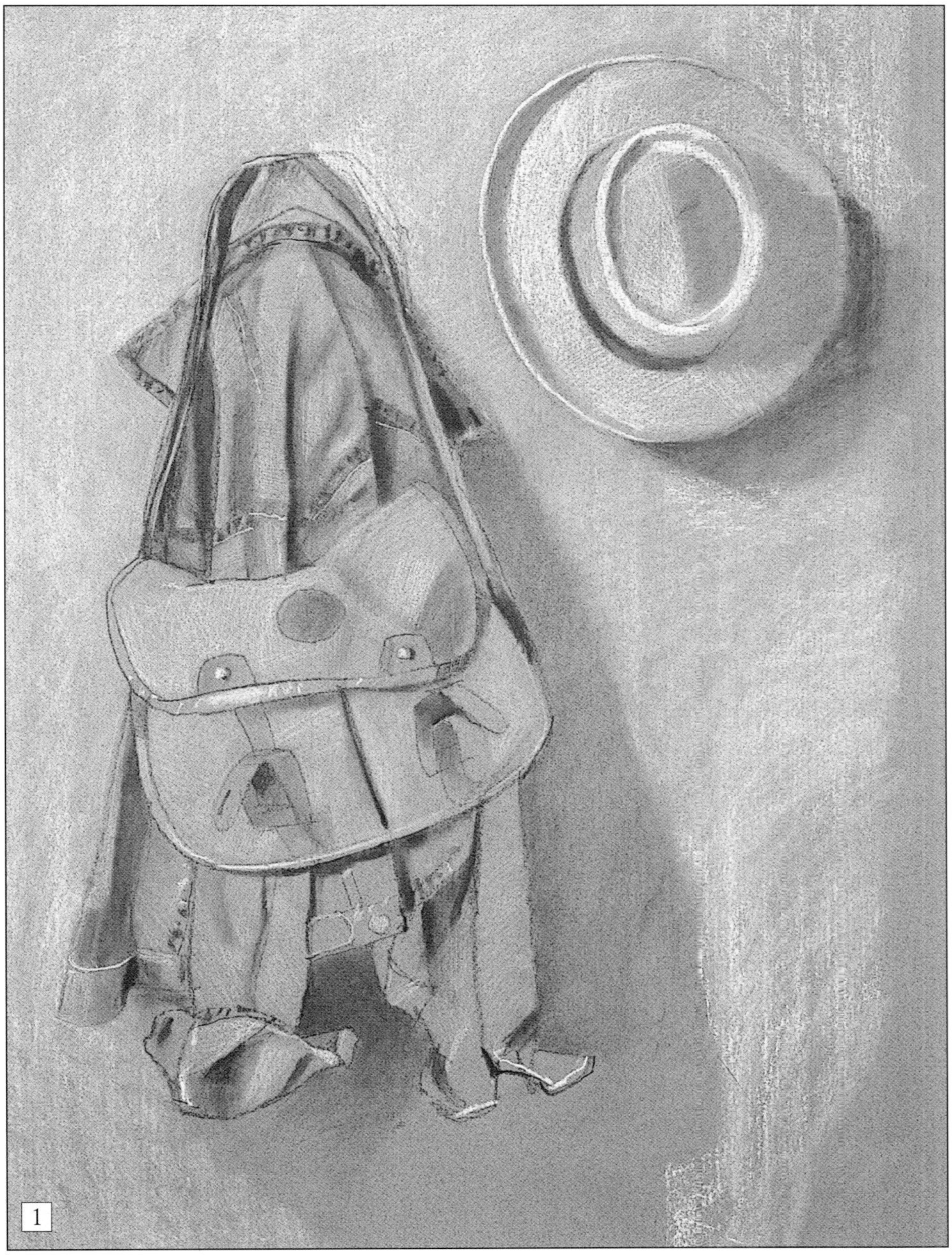

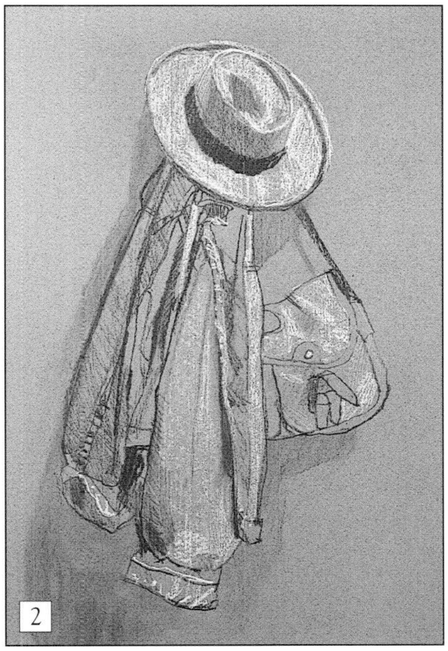

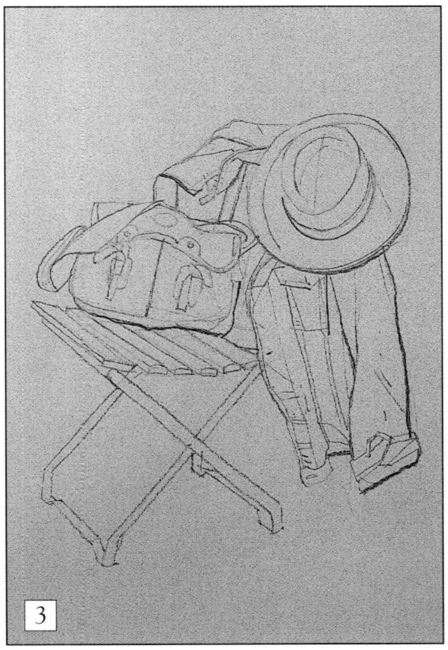

**1** The composition has been changed so that the bag hangs on top of the jacket and the hat is off to one side by itself. This positioning suggests that, spatially, the bag sitting on top of the jacket is nearer the viewer than the hat, and we read it this way although the hat is lighter in tone and seems to be more prominent.

**2** This drawing is much looser. It was done very quickly – in just a few minutes – while trying to decide on a pleasing arrangement, and was the first of the session. The range of tone is limited, with the white dominating, showing the direction of the light source. It is sometimes a good idea to do a so-called warm-up drawing; the fingers loosen up and the marks seem to flow easier after a few minutes scribbling.

**3** Adding a fourth element, the chair, increases the possible compostions, and inspires a carefully constructed, more considered drawing in line only.

# PORTRAIT

*Conté Pencil*

PROJECT SIX

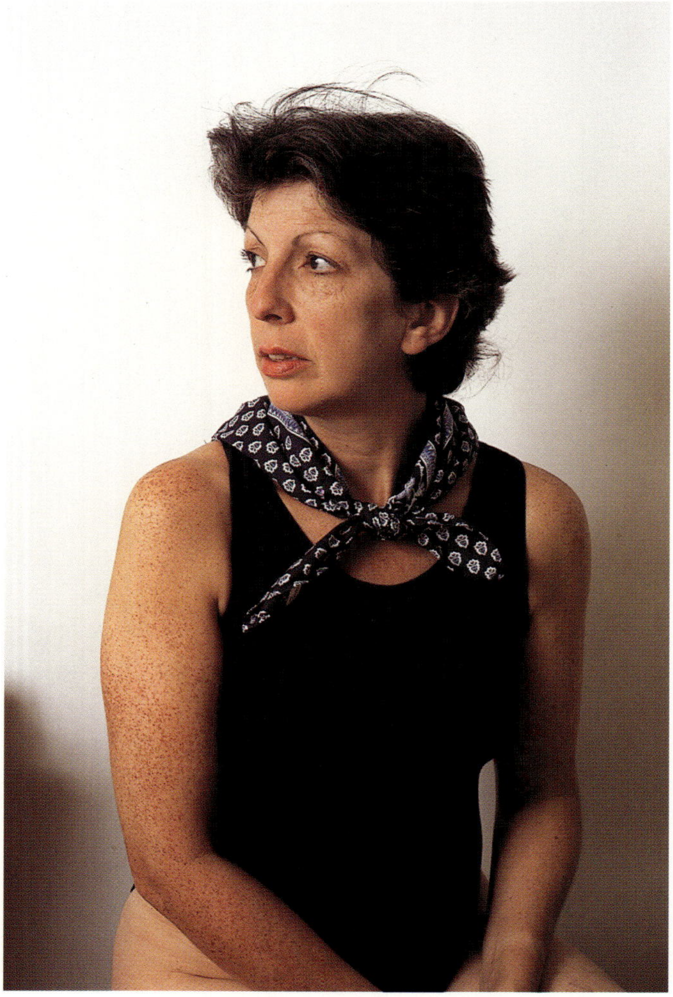

THE PORTRAIT HAS always been considered the most difficult subject for the artist – along with hands and feet, and closely followed by the human figure. When we objectively draw or paint most other things a certain degree of latitude seems to be acceptable. What does it matter if two or three trees are left out of a wooded landscape, or five instead of six oranges are drawn in a still life? In fact this visual editing of what we see and choose to put on paper should and does happen all the time, as artists use licence to improve on composition and design. But draw a portrait wrong and the world and his wife seem to notice.

## Materials and Equipment

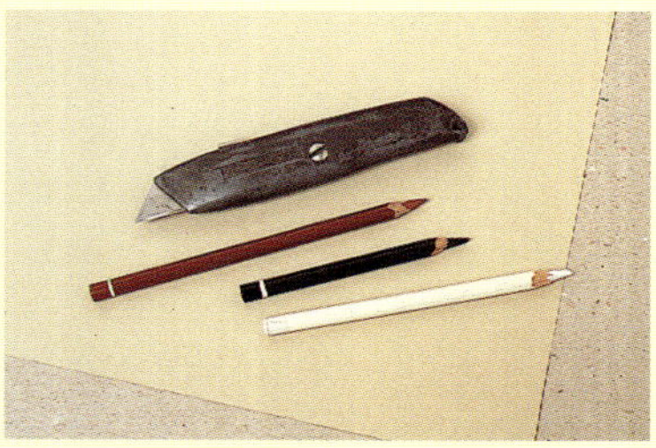

20x14 in sheet of cream-coloured Ingres paper
Stanley knife or craft knife
Conté pencils, black, white and sanguine or terracotta

It was the American portrait painter John Singer Sargent who referred to portraits as 'a likeness in which there is something wrong about the mouth'. Approach portraits as you would any other subject: get the basic proportions right; plan and position the features relative to each other correctly; make them look as if they are sitting convincingly on a firm structure – and a likeness will inevitably follow.

A useful formula for estimating proportion for portraits is the rule of halves. Put simply, the eyes tend to sit on a line about halfway between the top of the head and the chin; the bottom of the nose on a line halfway between the eyes; and the chin and the base of the lower lip on a line halfway between the nose and the chin. Obviously this should act as a guide only: proportions differ from person to person, but it will help to establish the approximate position of the sitter's features.

*Le trois crayon*, the three crayons, is a traditional drawing technique seldom used today but capable of producing seductive drawings of great depth and beauty. The technique is a useful exercise in controlling tone. Working on a light- to mid-toned paper a black crayon supplies the dark areas, a red or sanguine the mid tones and the white the highlights.

# The Drawing

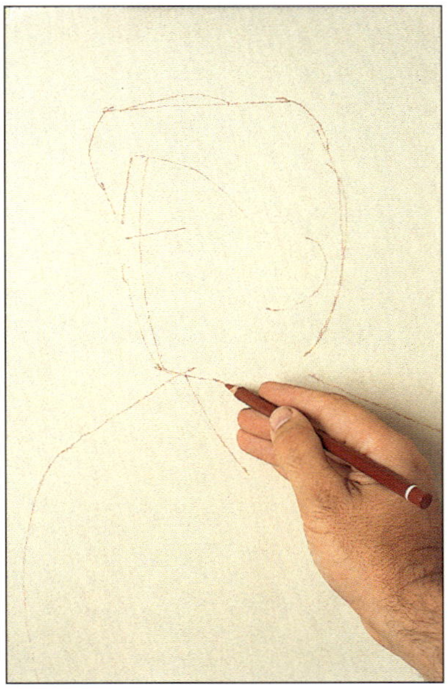

1 With a sanguine pencil, and using light marks, establish the position and axis of the head. Work out the height and width by making a few preliminary measurements, paying particular attention to the way the head is turned. This is indicated by marking the apparent position of the centre of the face – the imaginary line that, if the face is viewed from the front, would run down the middle between the eyes and the centre of the nose. On this line indicate the position of the nose and mouth and the angle of the eyes. Measure back across the head and position the ear. As a rule you will find that the top of the ear lines up with the eyes and the bottom with the mouth.

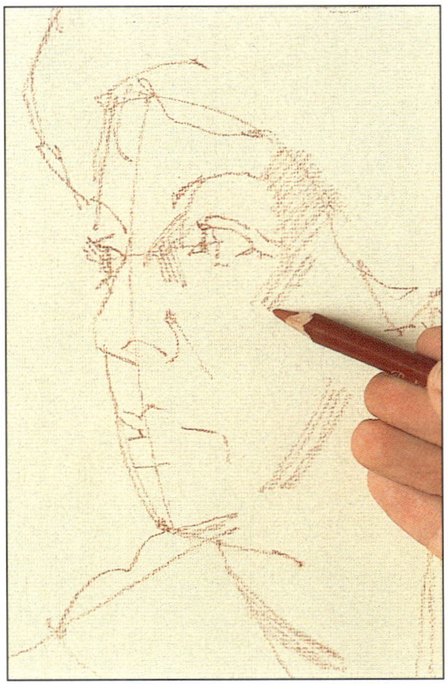

2 Making use of these few construction lines, which act as a guide, begin to draw the features in lightly. The light marks made with soft conté crayon, unlike those made with conté chalks, can be corrected easily by using a soft putty eraser. Loosely hatch on a little tone to indicate the side of the nose that is in shadow, and so indicate the direction of the light. At this point the drawing already begins to have depth as we look across the face into the drawing.

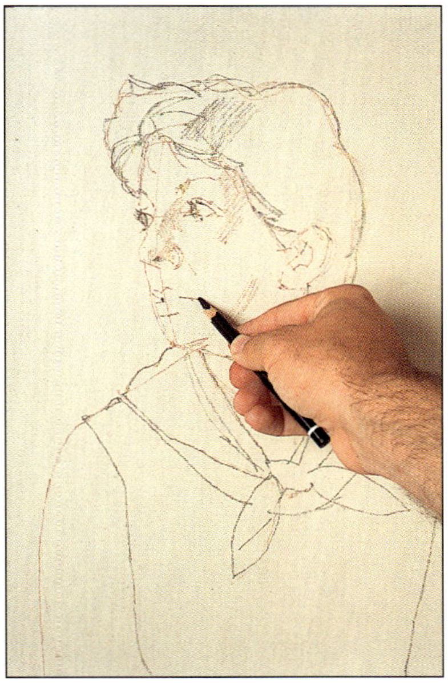

3 The black conté pencil is then used to darken the eyes and lashes; the shape and fall of the hair is redrawn and redefined, and the dark area inside the slightly open mouth is pencilled in. With loose, flowing lines draw in the scarf and top. Take care to make the clothes appear as if they fit on and around the figure by curving the pencil lines into and over the underlying form.

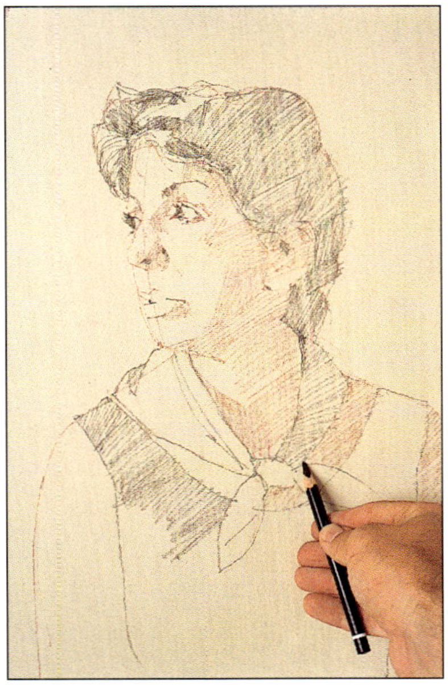

4 Take up the sanguine pencil and hatch in the areas of shade down the right-hand side of the face and neck, under the eye and down to the side of the mouth. With the black pencil darken the eyebrow, hatch in the hair, the scarf and the top. Do not make the hatching too dark; while it is easy to darken these areas by working over them again it is a more awkward task to lighten them. These loose areas of tone have the immediate effect of giving solidity to the form.

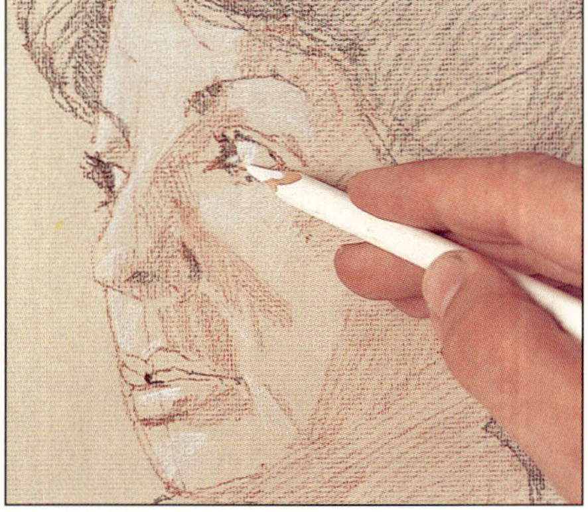

5 With the white conté pencil hatch in the light areas, paying particular attention to the white of the eye and the highlight on the lower lip.

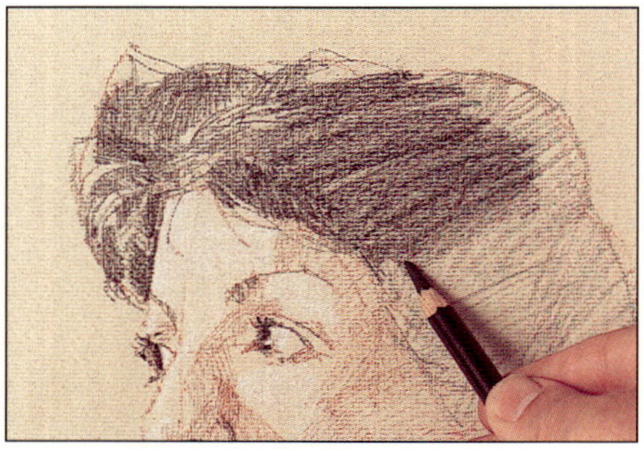

6 Rework the hair with the black conté, paying attention to the shape and suggesting here and there the detail of a few individual hairs. With the sanguine pencil shade in the top lip.

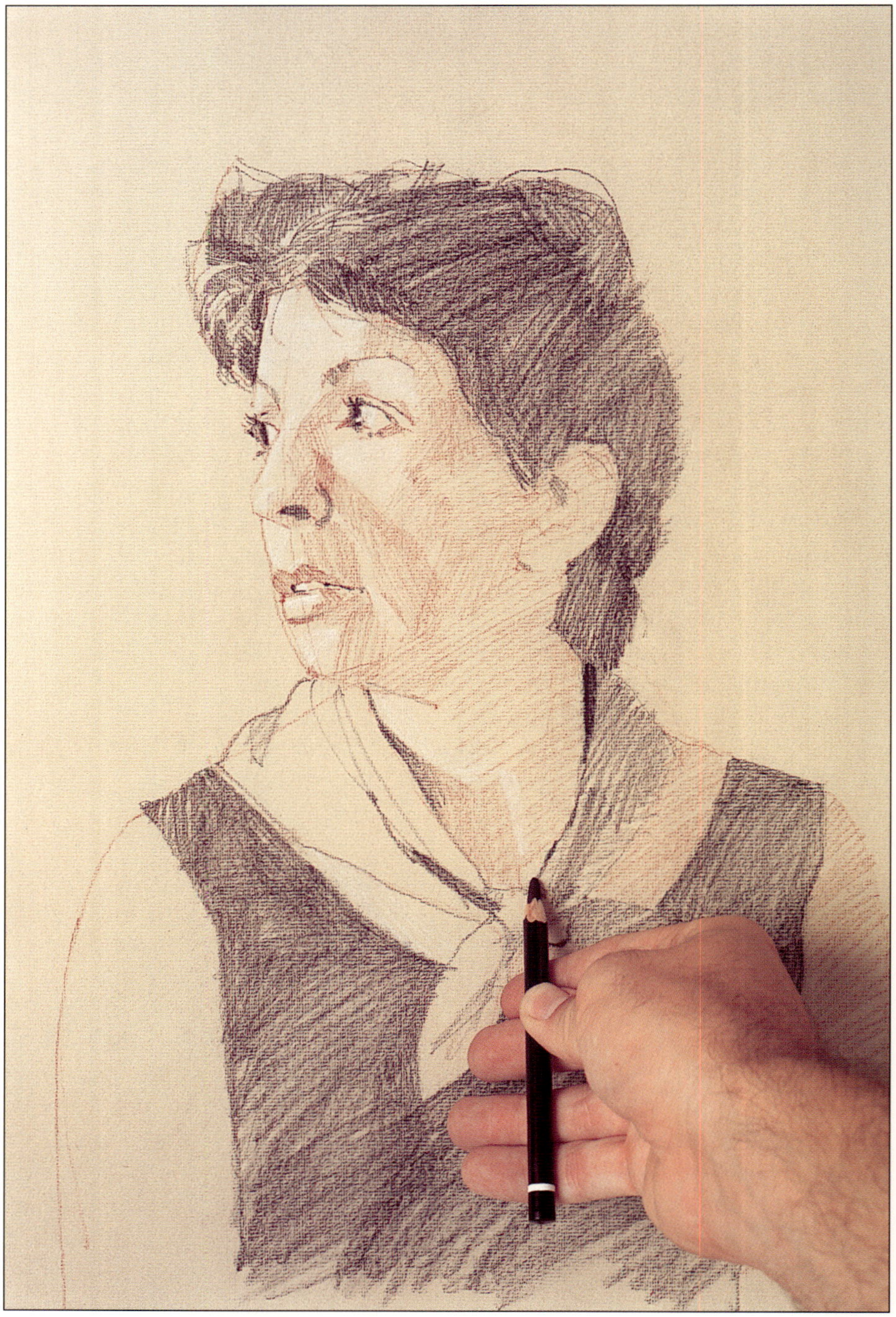

7 Darken the shadows on the scarf where it sits against the neck and rework the black top.

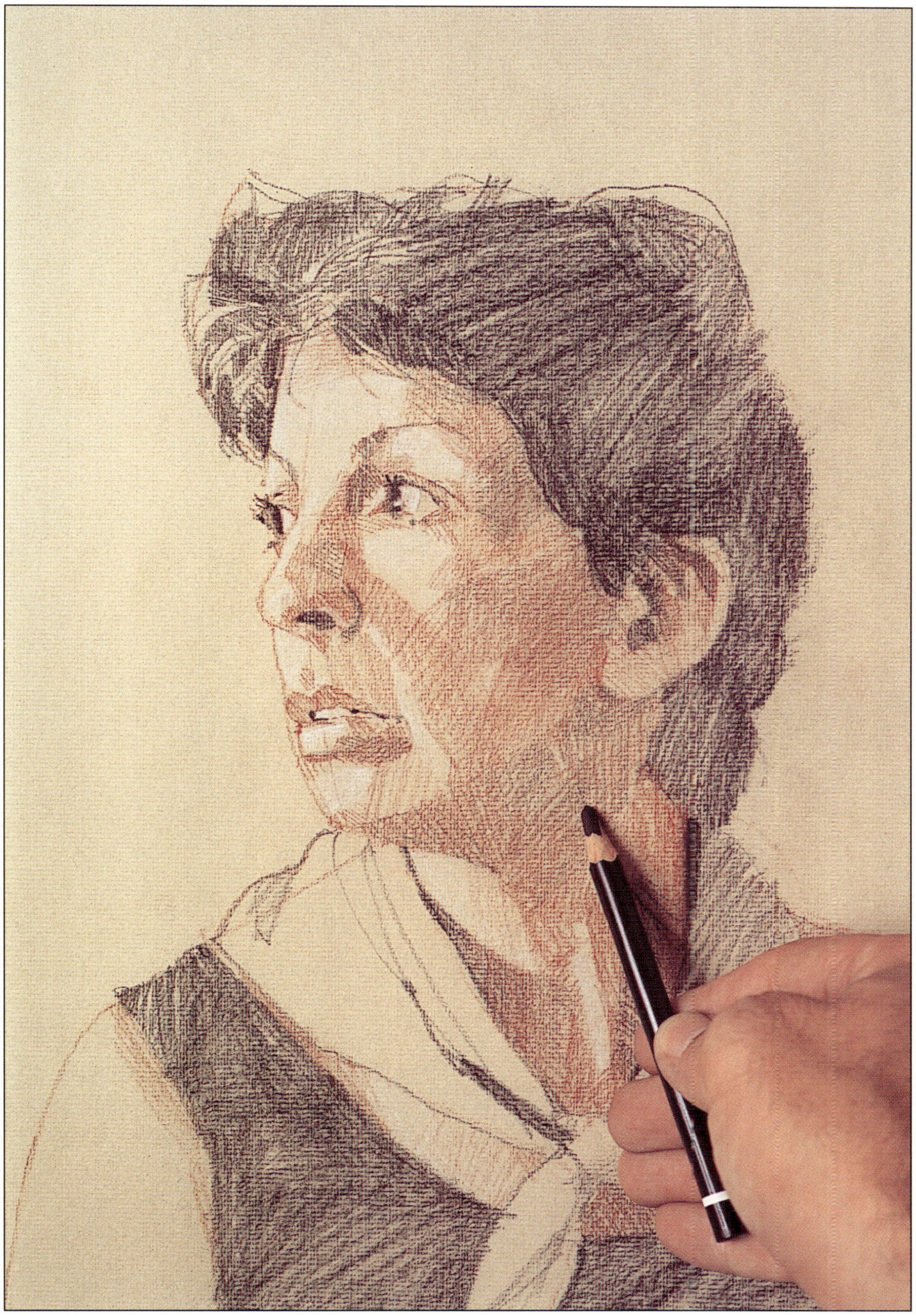

8 With the sanguine and the black conté pencils methodically work across the face, adjusting the tones by cross-hatching and gradually building up the contours. The task will be easier and more precise if you keep your pencils sharpened to a point.

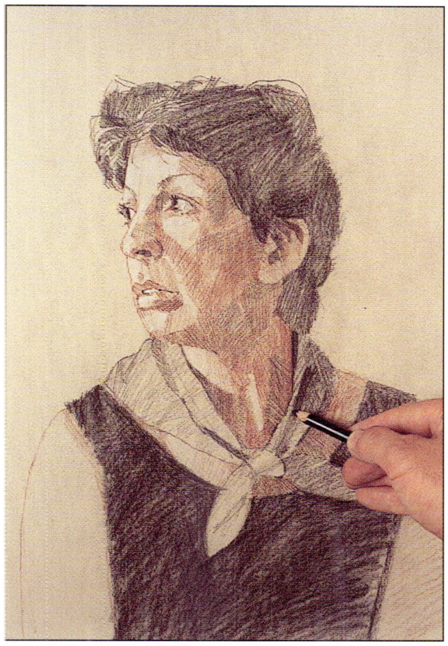

9 The neck scarf and top are darkened again. A light tone is loosely hatched over the lighter side of the scarf to separate it tonally from the background and help position the scarf on and around the neck.

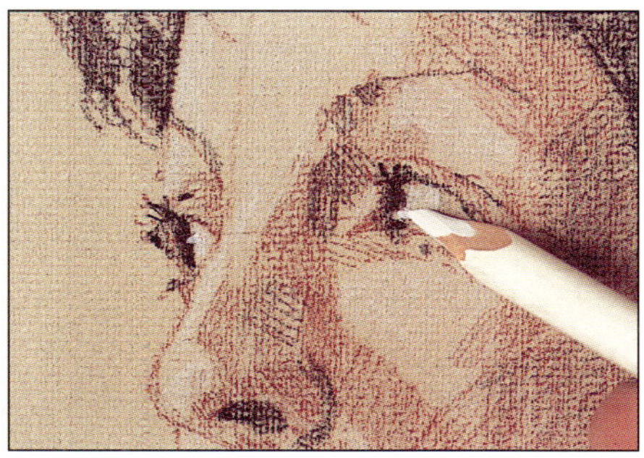

10 With a sharp white conté pencil press the highlights into the eyes.

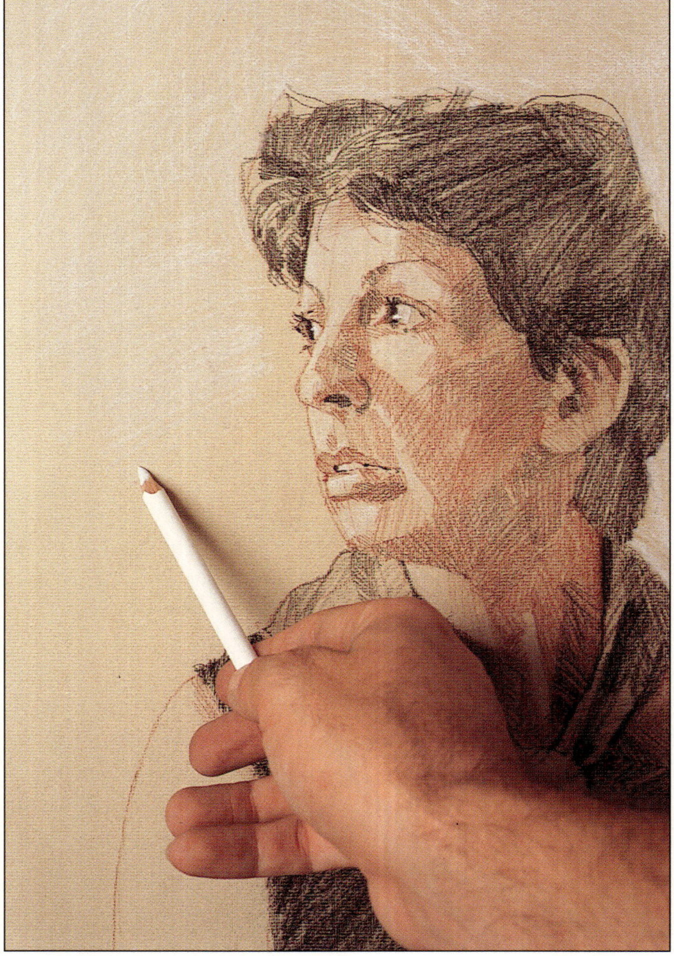

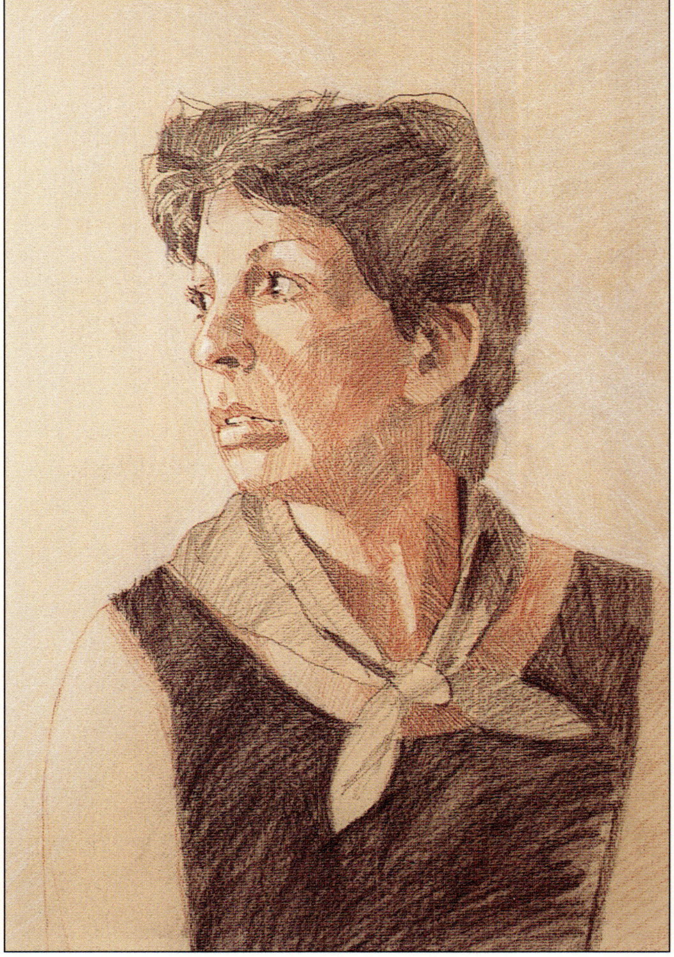

11 The background is lightened by scribbling over it with the white pencil, varying the direction of the strokes. This has the effect of lifting the head and visibly pushing it forward, out and away from the background.

12 The drawing receives a few adjustments and is finished. The three conté pencils and the cream-coloured paper have worked together to produce a deceptively colourful drawing.

# Alternative Approaches

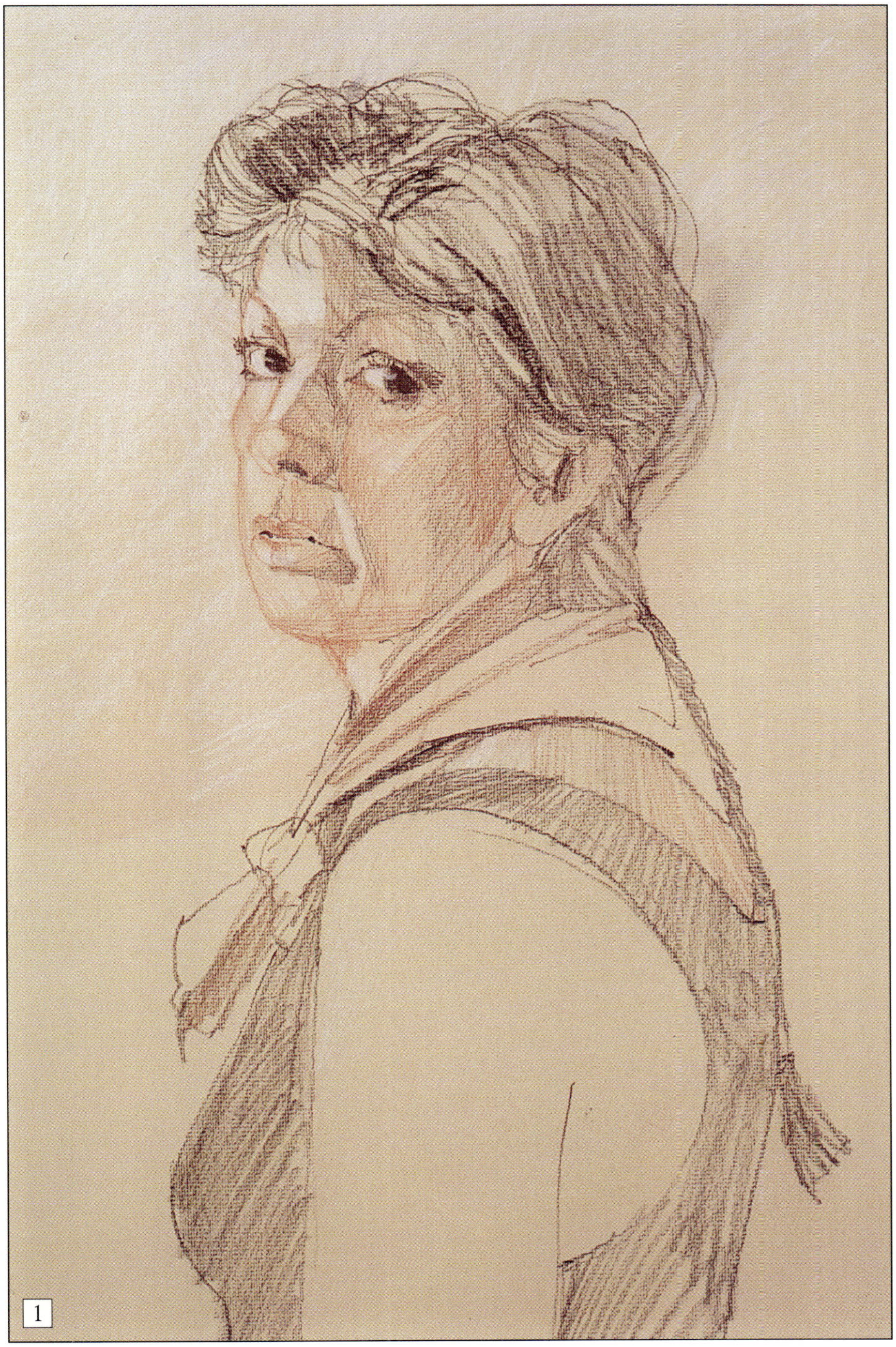

1

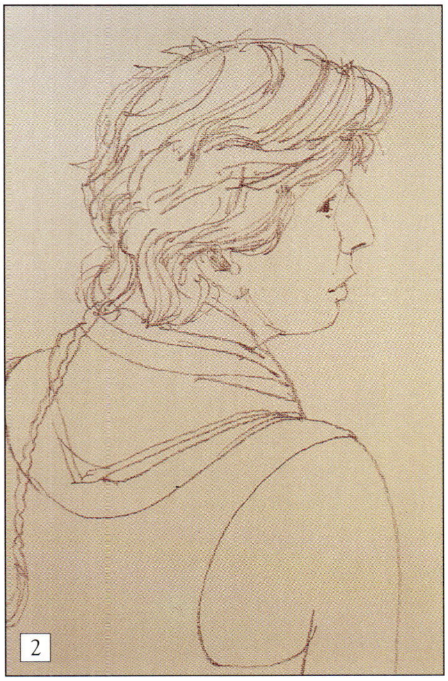

2

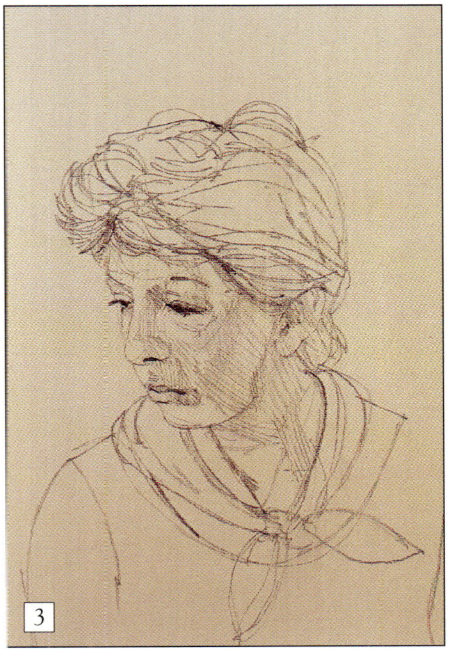

3

**1** The technique of using the three crayons remains the same but the drawing is looser, relying more on line to suggest the fall of the hair.

**2** Dark brown, rather than black, was used to give a dense line that was not too overpowering.

**3** A sharpened square black conté crayon gave a looser and more subtle line, with just a suggestion of hatching on the planes of the face, which gives just a hint of form.

# LOBSTER AND LEMONS

*Pen and Ink*

PROJECT SEVEN

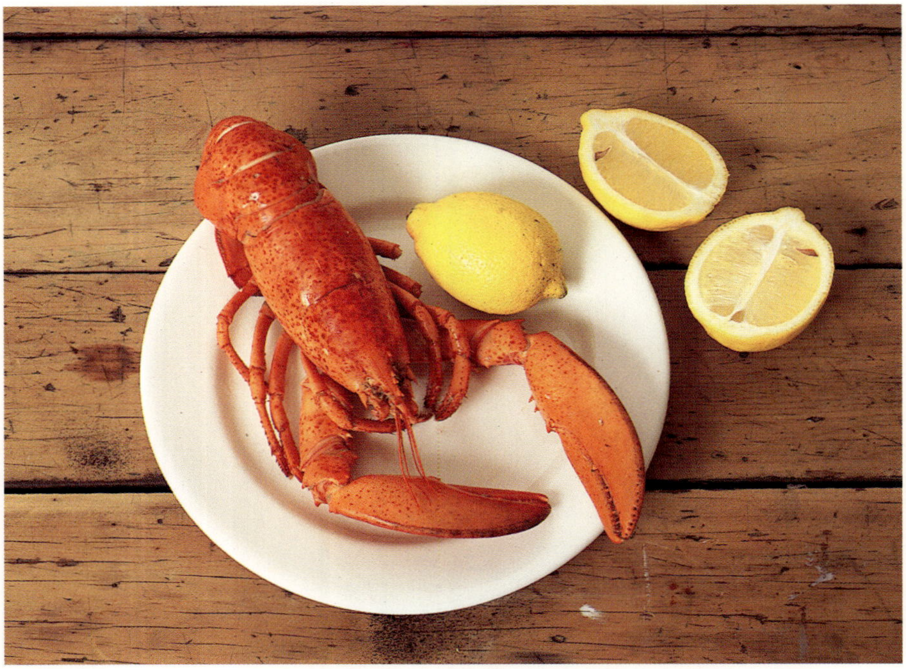

PEN-AND-INK techniques, much favoured today by illustrators for their clarity in reproduction, are well tried and have a fine tradition – they were a favoured medium of so many great artists of the past. Today, however, ink as a medium is often viewed with some trepidation by beginners – perhaps because it is seen as an unforgiving medium. While there is some truth in this attitude, a little planning and a little forethought should ensure that some of the potential problems will be avoided.

Pen-and-ink drawings are essentially about line. When used on a dip pen straight from the bottle the ink delivers a black of uniform density. It is the variation in line quality, the alternating combination of thick and thin, broken and continuous, hesitant and incisive, that give the medium its special quality.

The range of marks possible from a single nib are many, and it is perfectly possible to produce a drawing full of line, and with a variety of marks, using one nib only. The versatility of ink expands even further when you consider that, unlike all other drawing media, it is a liquid capable of being diluted, spattered, blotted, brushed, stippled and dribbled.

The lobster, along with other crustaceans, seems to have been created as the model for pen-and-ink drawings. Its contoured, segmented body, its long arms and legs covered in spines and nodes, demand the use of a wide repertoire of marks.

## MATERIALS AND EQUIPMENT

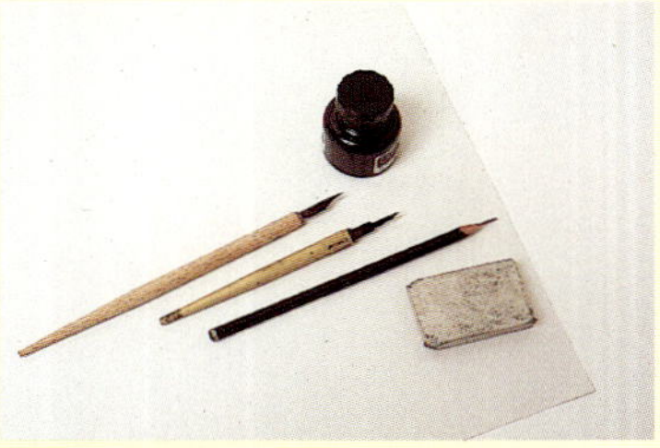

- Sheet of 200lb Not watercolour paper
- Two pen holders
- One thin nib and one thicker nib
- Waterproof Indian ink
- 2B pencil
- Putty eraser

# The Drawing

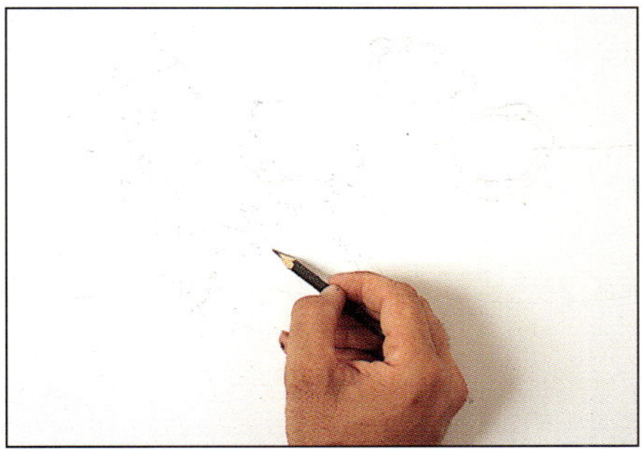

1 Lightly sketch in the lobster, plate and lemons with a soft pencil. There is no need to go into great detail, but include enough to act as a guide for the ink drawing. The pencil will be erased when the drawing is finished and the ink is dry. Don't press too hard or you will make indentations in the paper.

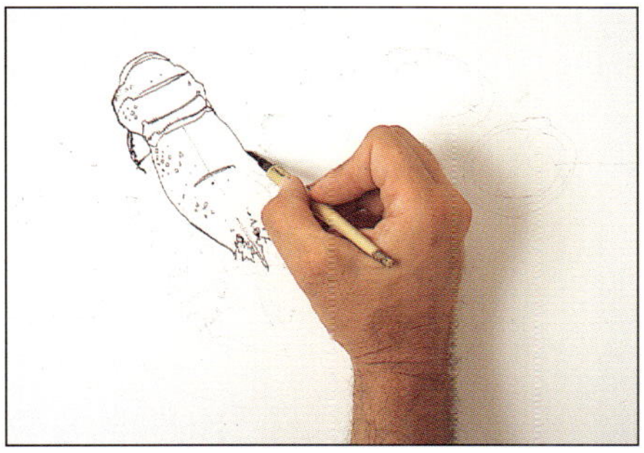

2 Begin to draw in the body of the lobster, working away from the drawn area so you don't smudge the wet ink. Use the pencil drawing as a guide but do redraw, referring constantly to the subject, rather than just following the pencil lines.

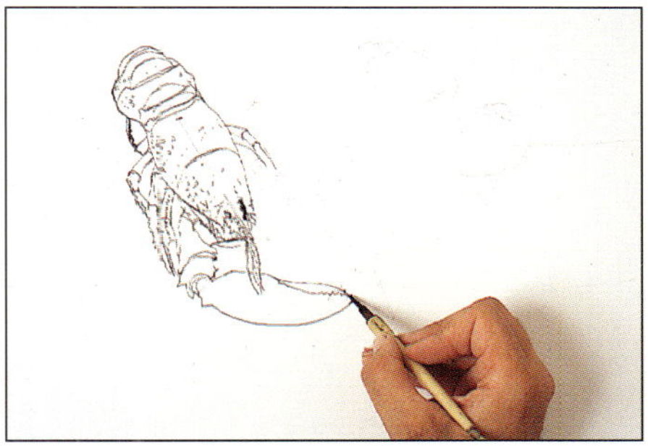

3 Work around the edge of the lobster. Press harder on the pen and splay the nib to get a thicker line: turn the nib on its side to obtain a very fine line. A line varying in thickness is central to pen-line drawing: the thicker lines suggest an edge that is in shadow, while a fine line suggests one that is brightly lit. Return periodically to indicate texture and pattern on the lobster's shell.

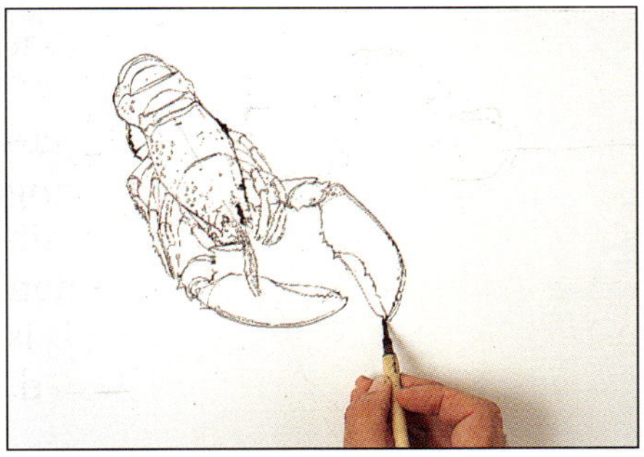

4 Long fluid lines indicate the shape of the claws. The light preliminary pencil drawing is especially useful for guiding these descriptive lines, which otherwise can be difficult to judge.

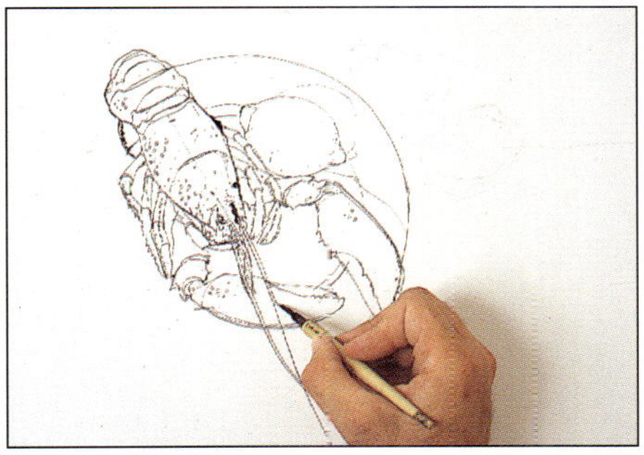

5 Draw in the lemon with a thin line that complements its delicate colour, indicate the far, curving edge of the plate, and the long antennae. The very observant will notice that my lobster had lost his antennae, so I indulged in a little artistic licence.

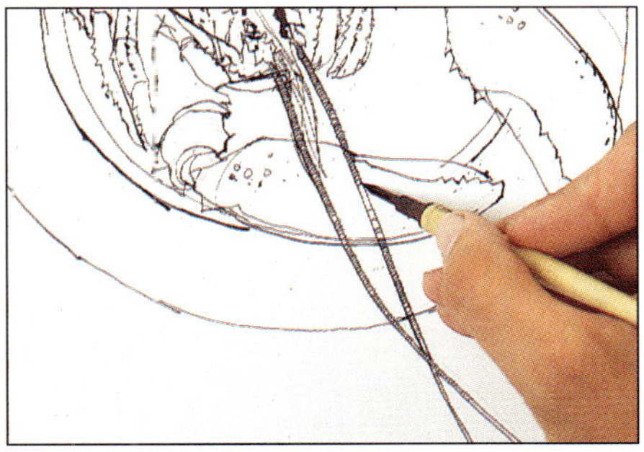

6 Finish drawing in the thin segment ridges that would make up the antennae, and finish the line of the plate. Note how a thicker line denotes the shadow on the inside edge.

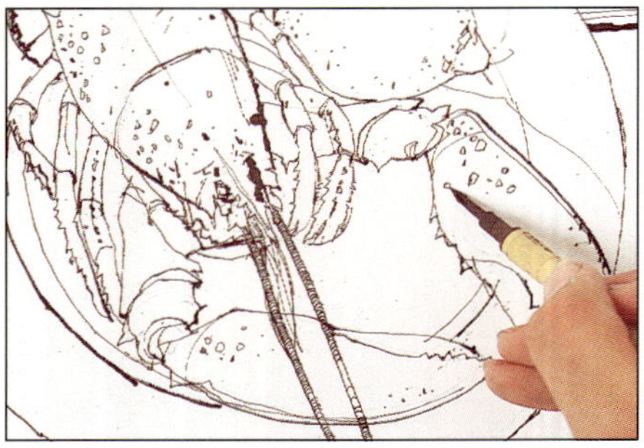

7 Dots and circles indicate the patterns and the textures on the lobster's shell.

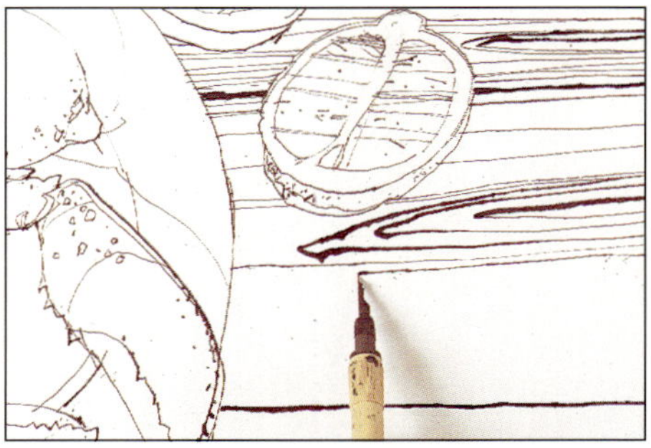

8 Draw in the two lemons on the table and the grain of the wood. Use plenty of ink on the nib and alternate long, light, fluid strokes – with the pen held well back from the nib – with short, heavier ones. The pen may catch on the paper, giving the line a jagged, broken look. Use the thicker pen nib for the thick, heavy lines.

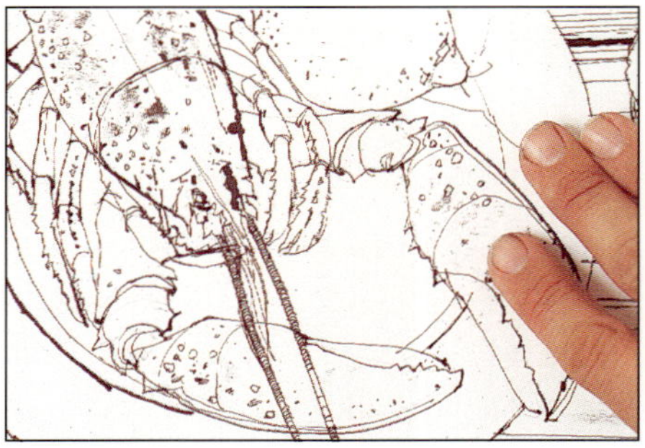

9 Touch the back of the nib with a finger or thumb and create texture on the shell by using your fingertip or tip of your thumb.

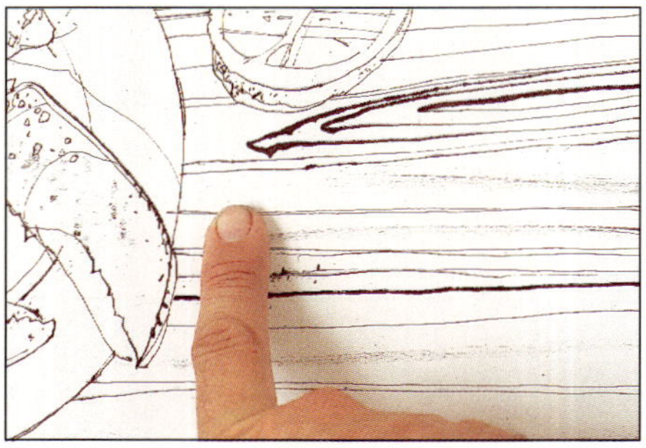

10 Dragging an inky finger over the surface of the paper creates a wood-grain-like smear.

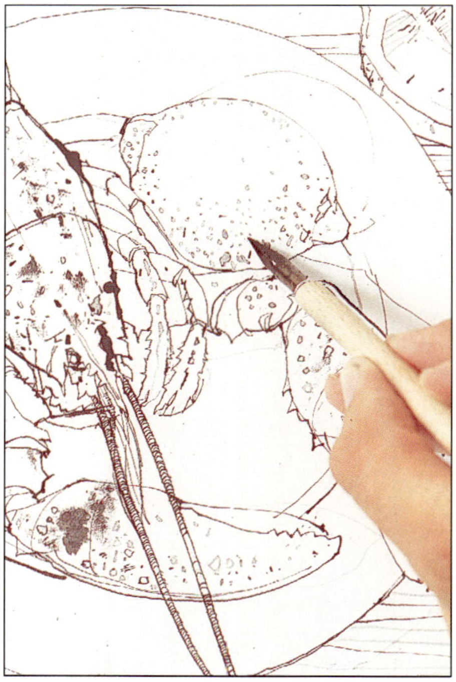

11 Dilute the ink with water for a subtle tone. Add the dilute ink to the nib with a brush (do not overload the nib as the thinned ink is prone to blob) and work back over the shell, creating more pattern and texture. Alternate between the thick and thin pen nibs in order to vary the marks.

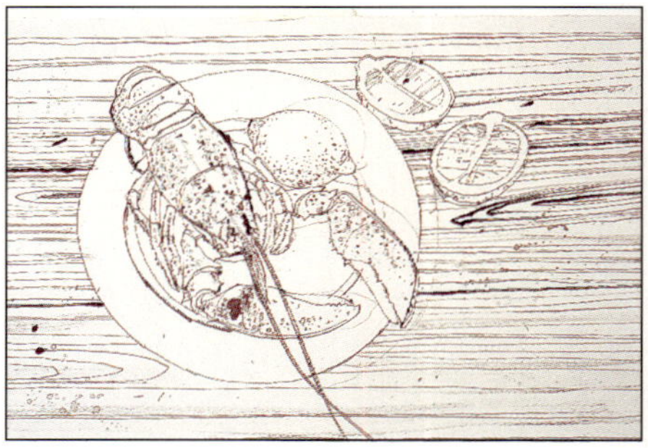

12 When the drawing is complete, allow it to dry overnight before attempting to erase any of the pencil drawing lying underneath, or you run the risk of smudging the ink.

# Alternative Approaches

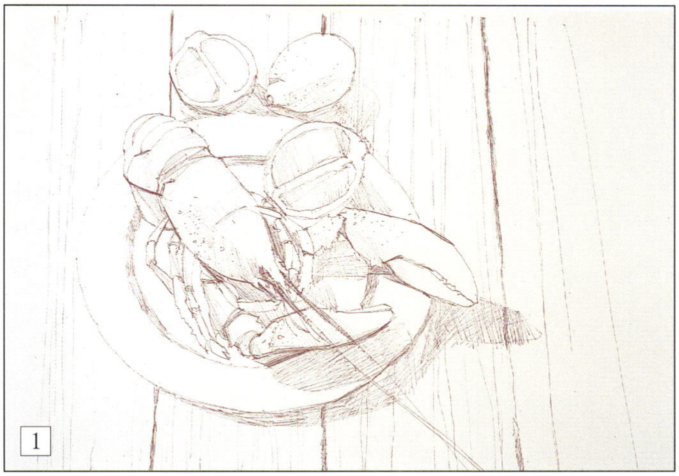

1

**1** An inexpensive, disposable, black biro was used for this drawing. While it is impossible to vary the thickness of line noticeably, it is possible to make the line lighter or darker by varying the pressure and the speed at which it moves across the surface of the paper.

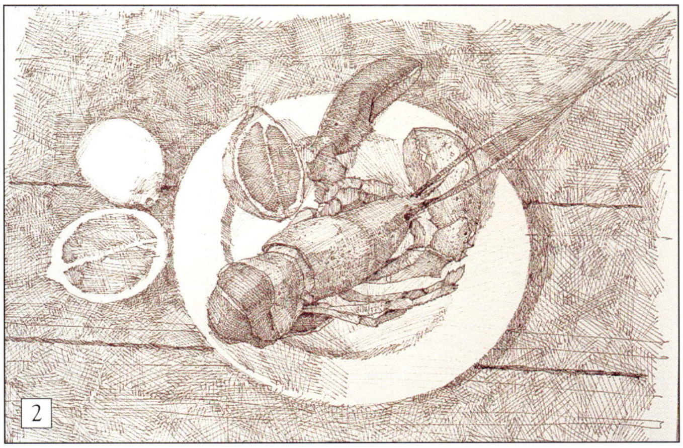

2

**2** This cross-hatched drawing was built up steadily using a fine technical pen. The same result could be achieved by using a fine liner or fine fibre-tipped pen. Notice how the density of the hatching gives the tone density. The lightest tone on the plate was made by using a pen that had almost run out of ink, and was only capable of making a light line.

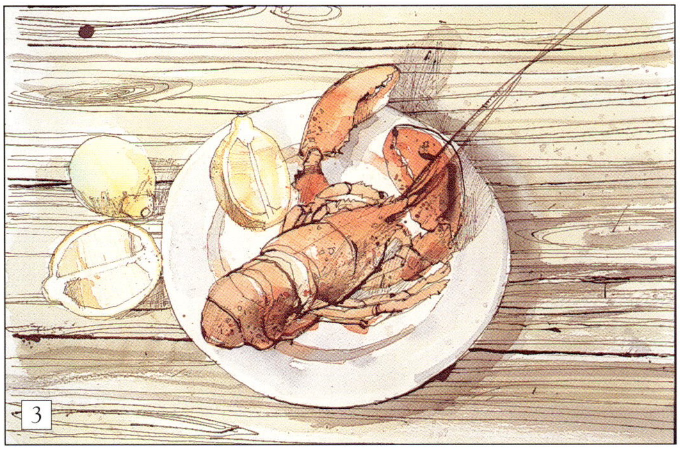

3

**3** Mixing waterproof and non-waterproof inks, and using watercolour – applied with brush and pen – pushes the possibilities further. The sharp pen line works well with the softer layers of tone and colour brushed loosely over the finished drawing.

# SUNLIT FIGURE

*Pen and Wash*

PROJECT EIGHT

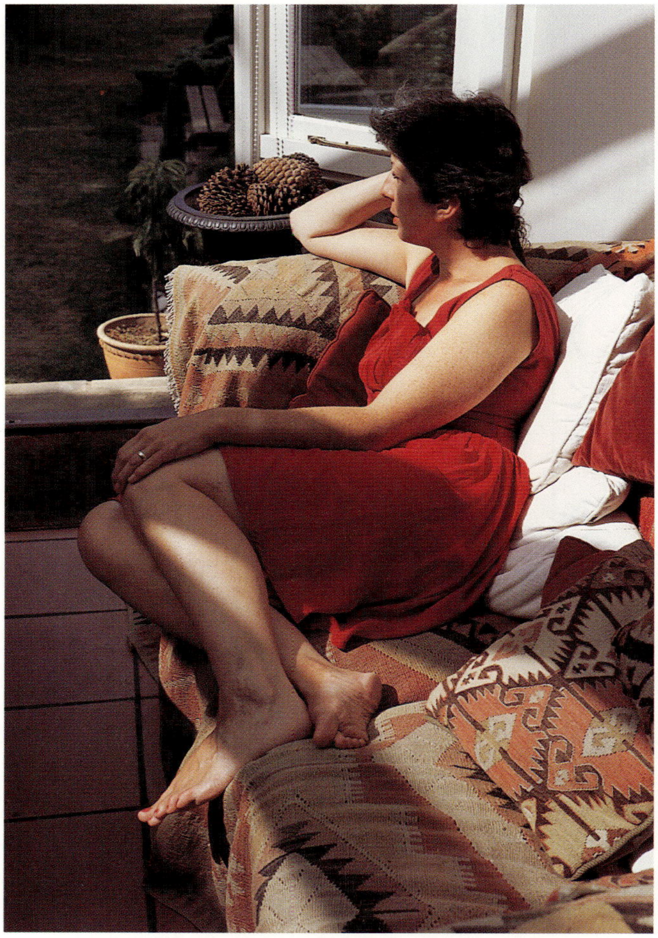

DILUTING INK WITH water immediately creates a more versatile medium. Tone can now be achieved with washes – rather than having to rely on the constraints that are inevitably found when depicting tone by stippling, hatching, cross-hatching and other techniques using line only. The two methods of working are often used together: the tones, light and shade, are created with a combination of wash and line; or by using the washes to show tone and colour while using line to describe the texture, the outline and the detail.

Whether you are using waterproof or non-waterproof inks, the wash techniques are very similar to those used when painting in watercolour. Watercolour is worked from light to dark, the darkest tones and colours usually being applied last. Ink washes are worked in the same way, as it is impossible to lighten a wash once it has been applied and is dry. This means that, as with watercolour, a little forethought and preliminary planning are required before beginning work.

Look at the subject and try to simplify what you see, grouping tones together, increasing the contrast between the lightest and the darkest. As we have mentioned before, looking at the subject through half-closed eyes will help, as this cuts down on detail and seems to reduce the perceived range of tone.

For this project, if you are not entirely confident you can make a very light preliminary pencil drawing as a guide. However, unlike the preliminary sketch that helped in the drawing of the lobster, it will not be possible to erase this one because the dry washes of ink will cover up the pencil marks. With the darker washes the tone of the wash will hide any pencil marks, but in those areas where the washes are very light the pencil marks may show through. Remember that once a wash is dry it will not be possible to lighten it – only to make it darker.

## MATERIALS AND EQUIPMENT

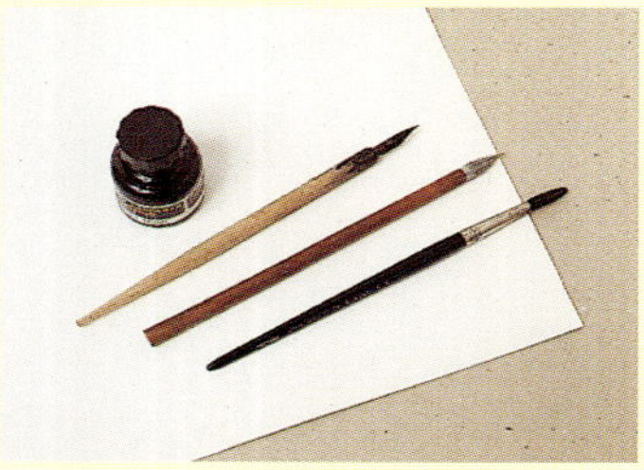

- One sheet of 22 x 15 in 300lb Not surface watercolour paper
- Black waterproof Indian ink diluted with water
- One nib of medium thickness
- One no 9 sable watercolour brush
- One medium-size Chinese brush

# The Drawing

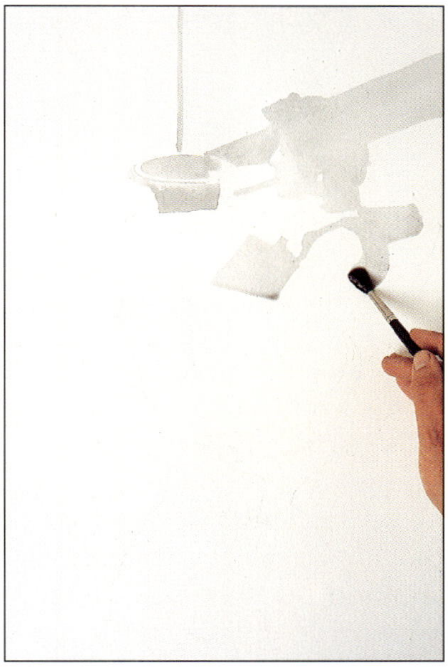

1 Mix a light to mid tone of ink and water. Working over a light HB-pencil drawing done as a guide, and beginning at the top of the paper, establish all the mid tone areas and the dark areas as one flat wash, using the no 9 sable brush. Be careful not to cover any light areas; if you do, you can quickly brush clean water on top and blot the resulting ink wash off with clean kitchen paper before the ink dries.

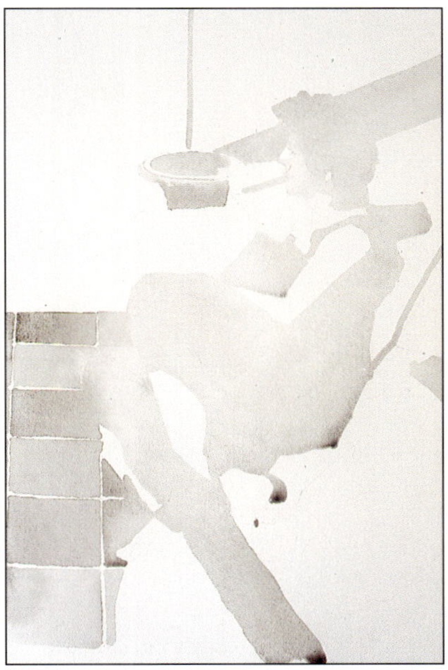

2 Continue to work down the drawing in the same way and indicate the lines of the stone floor tiles, the shadows across the legs and the cast shadow running over the couch. Working with the board at a slight angle means that the wet ink wash will puddle at the bottom of the drawing. Any excess ink can be removed by touching the puddle with a large dry brush or a piece of kitchen paper.

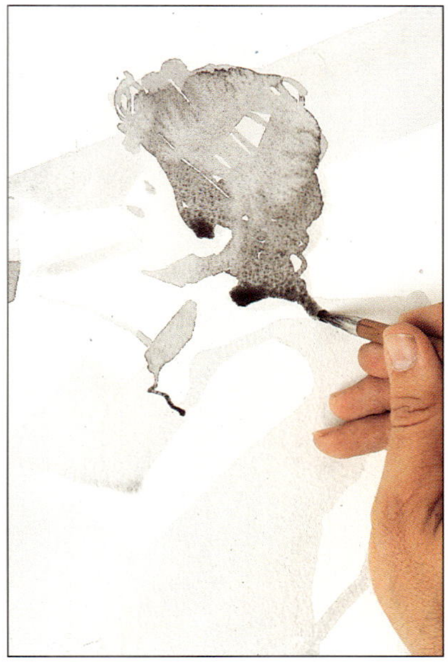

3 Allow the wash to dry. Mix a darker tone and, using the Chinese brush – which because of its shape gives a more expressive line – redefine the shape of the urn, the fall of the hair and the line of dark shadow at the front of the dress. Begin to put a little detail into the face by pulling the wash around to make the dark shadow beneath the chin. Darken the eye socket and the area below the nose.

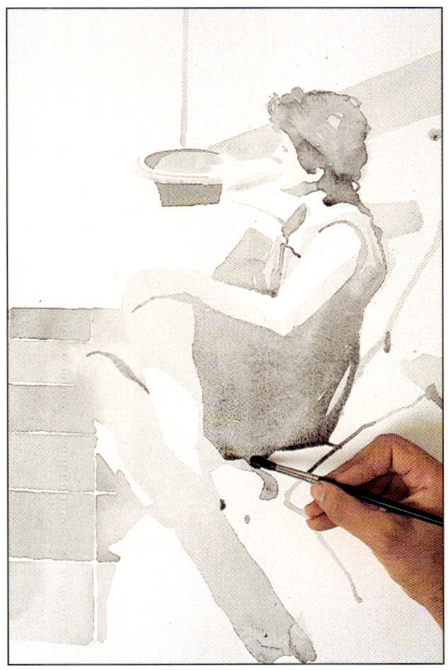

4 Block in the rest of the dress. Leave the areas where light catches the bodice and work carefully around the shape of the arm, indicating the shadow beneath the hand resting on the knee and the shadow of the dress draped across the other knee. While this is painted in one tone, if you allow the ink to 'puddle' in areas – for example on the hair, around the ear and the bottom of the dress – these areas wil dry to a darker tone. Before a wash dries it is also possible to flood water into it, making it lighter.

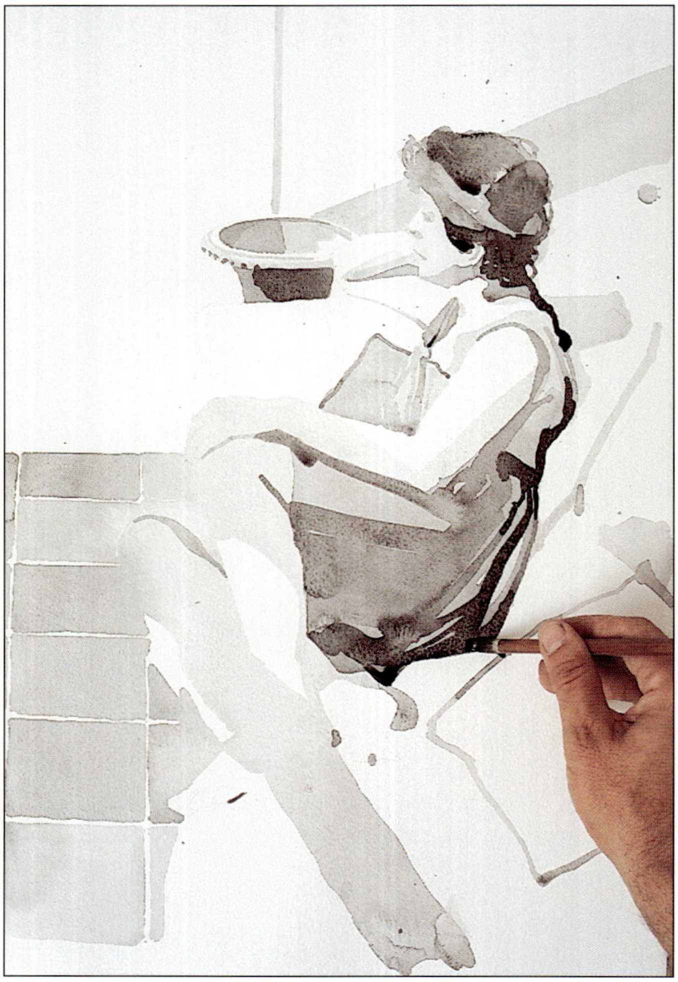

5 A little more ink is added to the previous mix to make it darker. Paint in the shadows on the urn, the darker tone found in the hair, the shadows in the creases and folds of the dress and the shadow beneath the arm resting on the knee. Allow the wash to dry slightly, then, working onto the still-damp paper, rework the back of the dress and some of the shadows, making them darker.

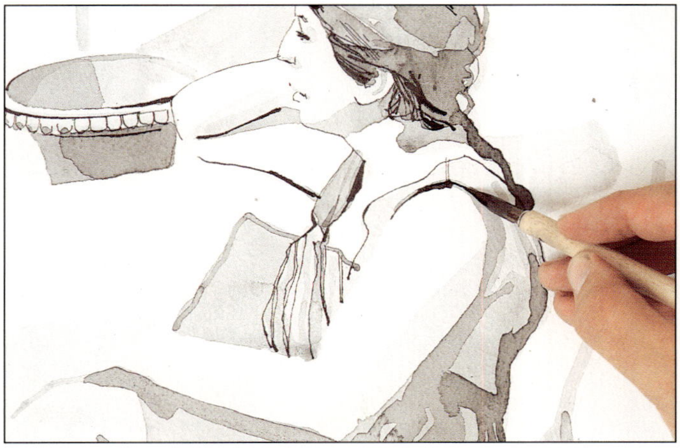

6 Once the washes are thoroughly dry the drawing is worked on in line, using the pen and undiluted Indian ink. Begin with the face, sharpening the features and the fall of the hair. Thin lines show the ruched material on the front of the dress, while lines that alter in thickness, indicating shadow, describe the arm and the shoulder. **Note:** Using a hair dryer will hasten the drying process, but do be careful not to blow dilute ink onto areas where it is not wanted.

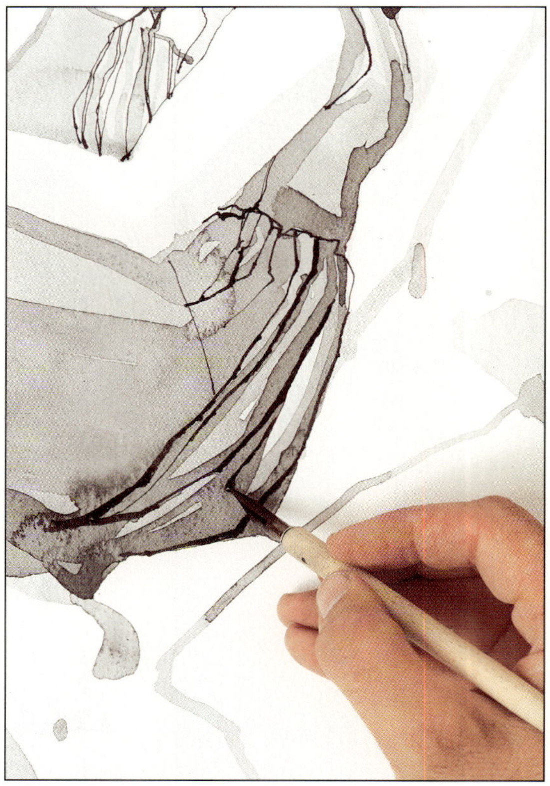

7 The back of the dress receives the same treatment as the front. By holding the pen near the nib you can apply the pressure necessary to make the lines thicker.

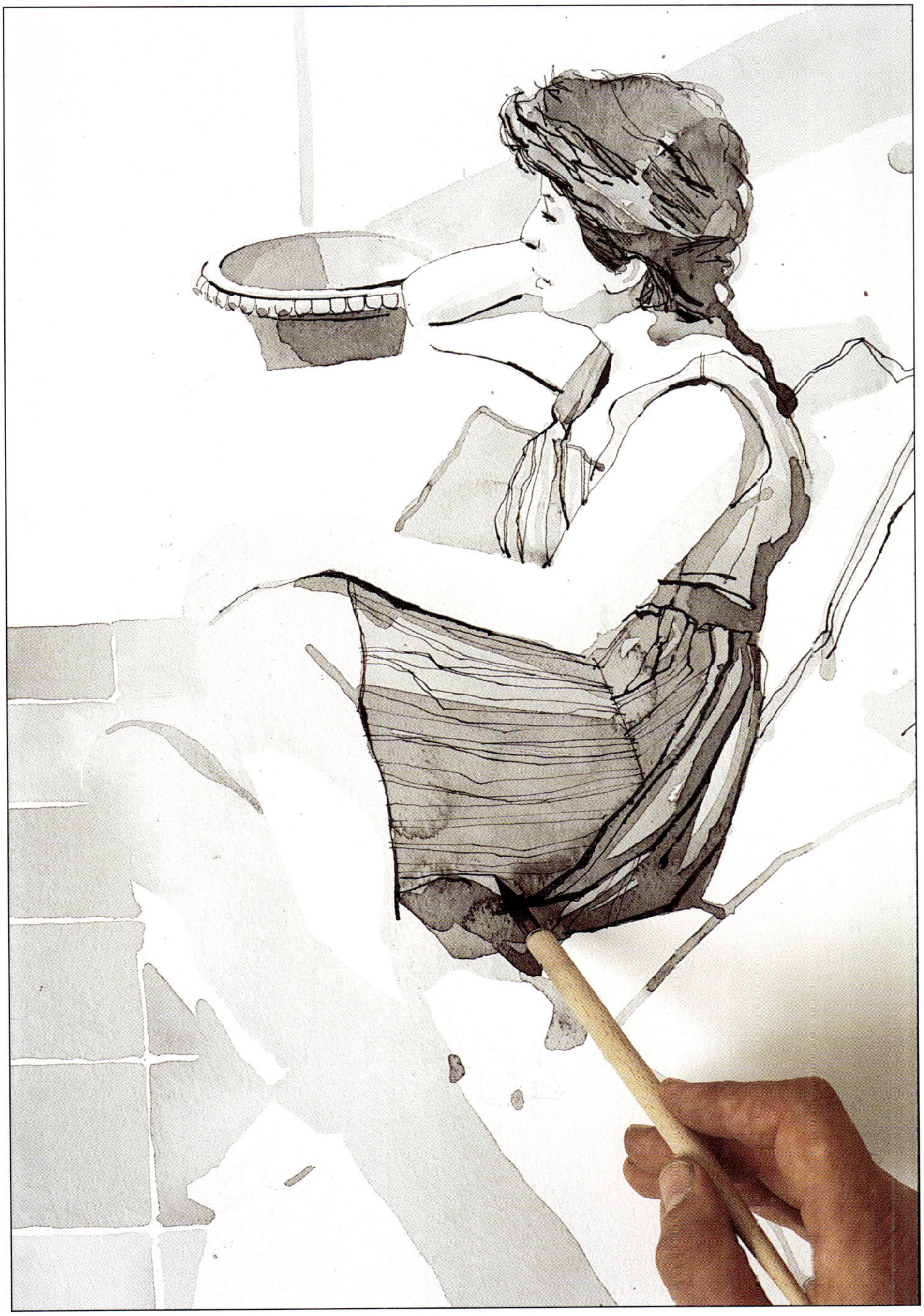

8 Holding the pen higher creates lighter lines, as less pressure is applied to the nib, restricting the amount of ink that flows onto the paper.

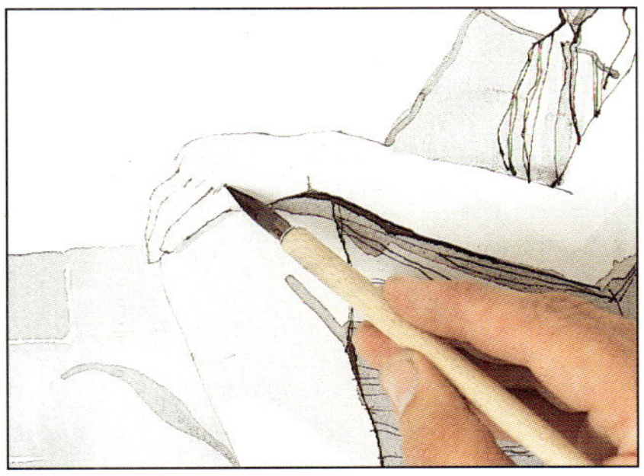

9 Dilute ink is used to draw the hands. The underlying drawing and the tone help position the lines correctly, while diluting the ink makes the line lighter and more delicate. Draw in the line of tassels on the edge of the kilim covering the couch.

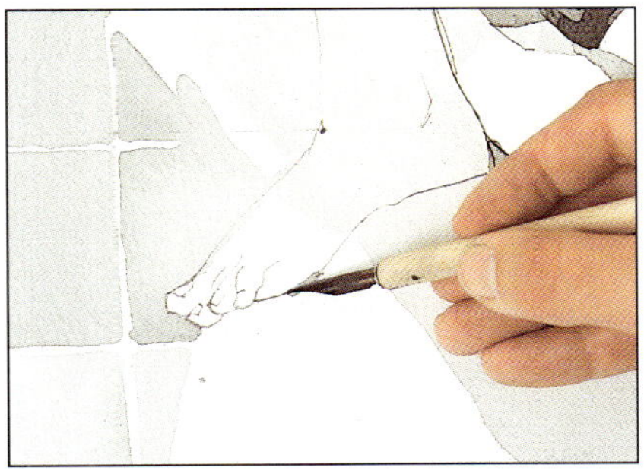

10 The feet receive the same treatment as the hands, again using dilute ink.

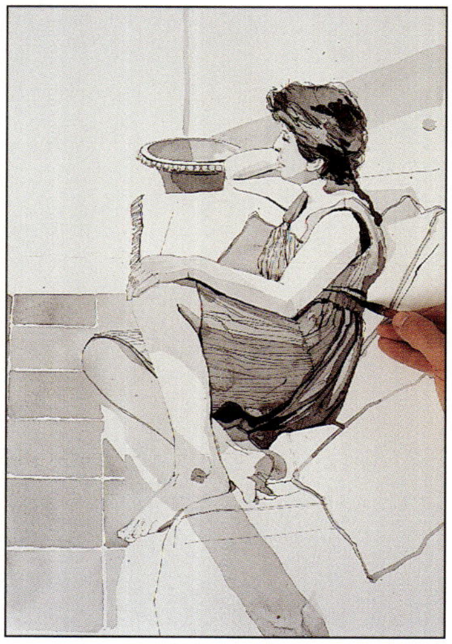

11 A light tone is used to modify the shadows on the hand and feet; a darker mix strengthens the hair and the deep shadows in the creases at the back of the dress.

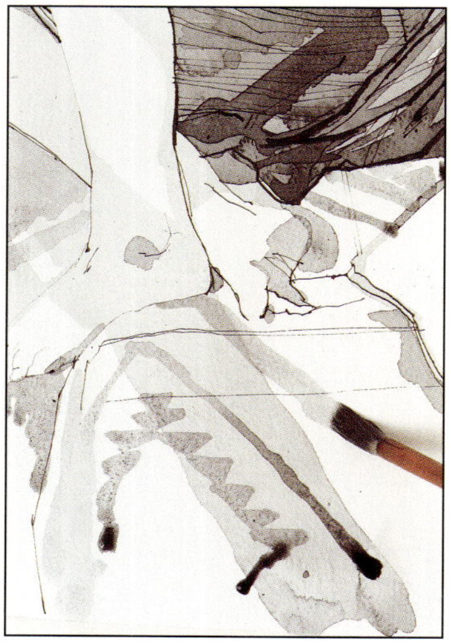

12 With varying tones of dilute ink the material of the dress is loosened up and the pattern on the kilim painted. Work loosely, but carefully follow the contours and folds, allowing the pattern to indicate the form of the couch.

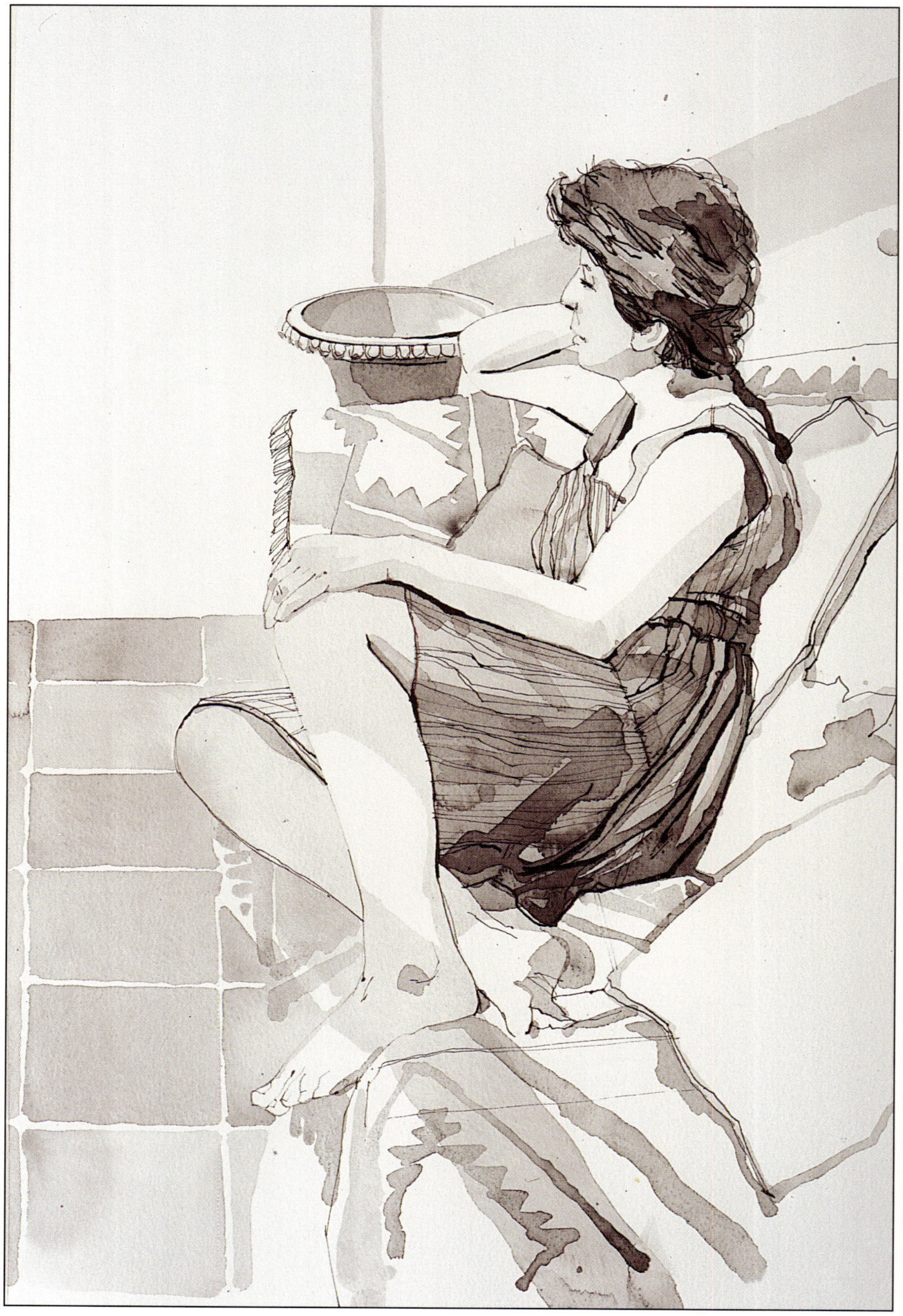

13 The finished drawing shows how the combination of line and bold washes work together, complementing each other and creating a strong image that nevertheless contains subtle variations in light and shade. The loose brush work on the dress and in the pattern of the kilim hints at the softness and texture of the material.

# Alternative Approaches

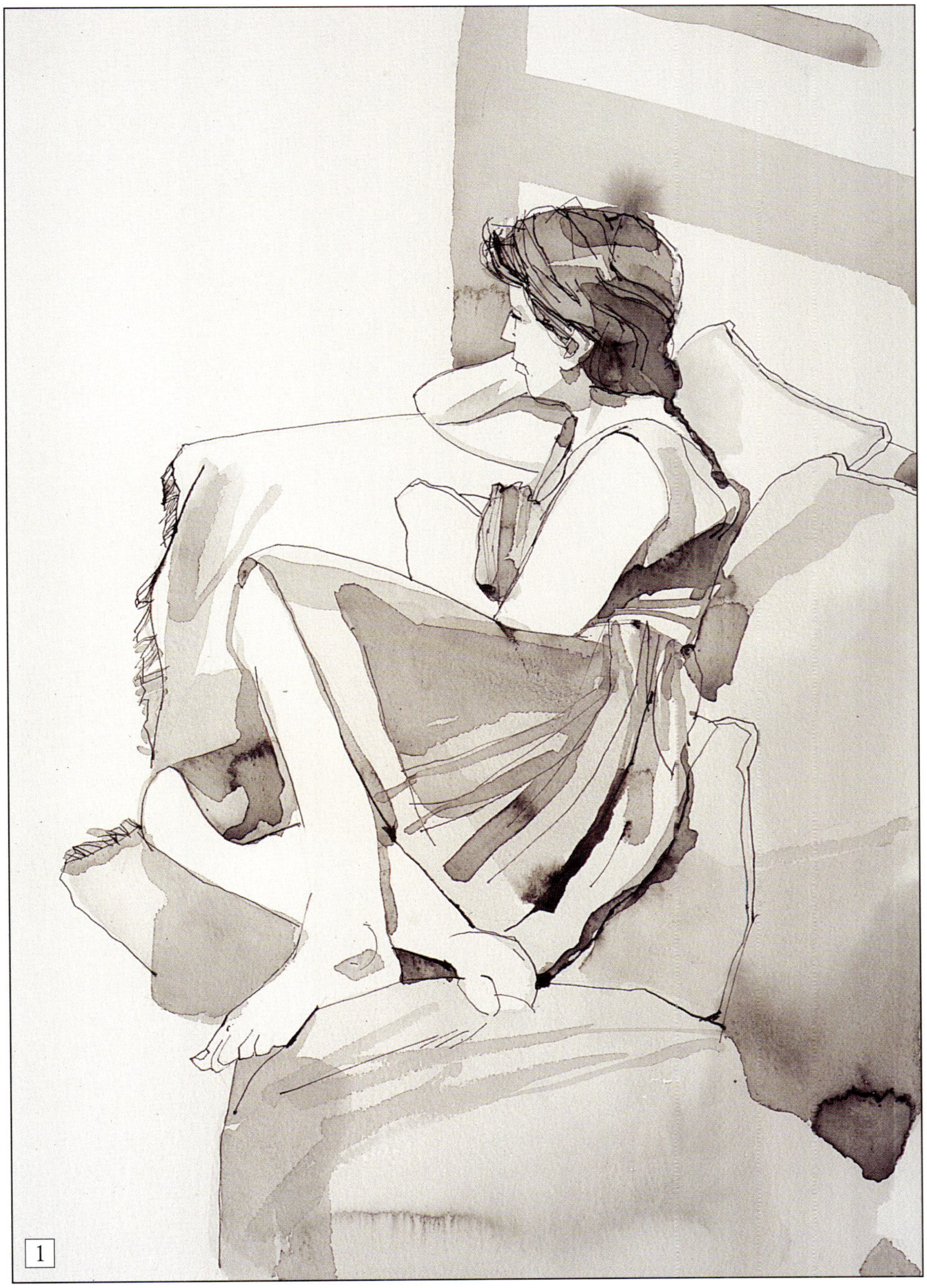

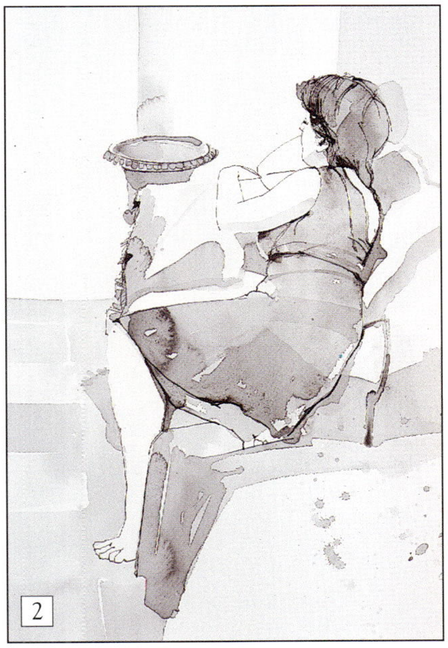

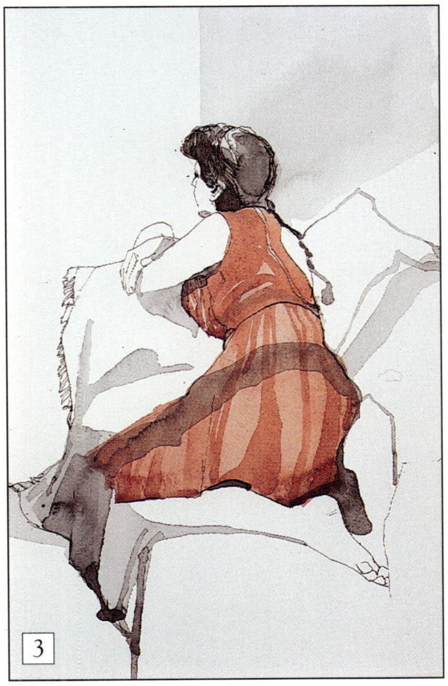

1 The same techniques of wash and line have been used in this composition, but with fewer and looser washes. The image was drawn in pen using waterproof ink. Later, when the ink was dry, washes were worked over the pen drawing. The image is simplified by leaving out the pattern on the couch and omitting the urn, thus putting greater emphasis on the shadows thrown across the wall behind the subject.

2 Loose, simple washes worked wet into wet are contained with just a few lines.

3 After the initial laying-in of light and shade a thin mix of dark red watercolour was used for the dress. The drawing was finished in line using waterproof ink. When the ink on the dress was dry this area was reworked using more of the same watercolour mix.

# THE VILLAGE CHURCH

*Pen, Wash and Gouache*

PROJECT NINE

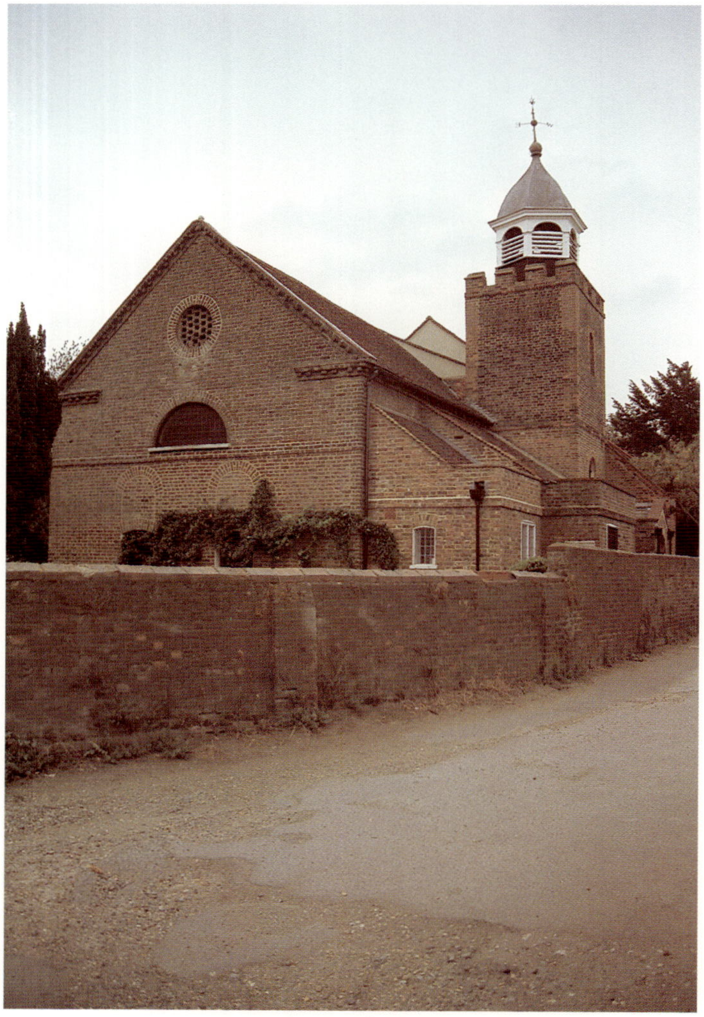

THE SUBJECT OF THIS project demonstrates how a number of different drawing media can be used to create new and exciting possibilities. Although certain combinations, such as charcoal and gouache, ink and watercolour, have long been favoured, there are no written rules to say what should and should not be used together,

Using a variety of artistic treatments in one drawing is particularly suitable for architectural subjects. The materials from which buildings are constructed often have marvellous texture and colour, and the shapes of the buildings, together with their surroundings, provide the artist with a wealth of suitable subject matter. The buildings themselves can also be particularly inspiring.

Old buildings, new buildings, small and large, all have something to offer. Churches especially seem to be a subject that artists return to again and again, and many of the older churches are situated where it is particularly pleasant for the artist to work on the spot.

In order for a building to stand, its construction must conform to certain geometric criteria. Linear perspective echoes these criteria, but this is a complex and involved subject – to deal with it in any depth is beyond the scope of this book. Put simply, the principle dictates that all receding parallel lines meet at a mutual point in space, a point known as the vanishing point. This point lies on the so-called horizon line, an imaginary line that runs horizontally and lies at eye-level, regardless of your position.

The drawing of a small village church on the outskirts of London offered the opportunity to use just a few different techniques and media in one drawing. Countless other, equally agreeable, combinations will be found simply by experimenting.

## MATERIALS AND EQUIPMENT

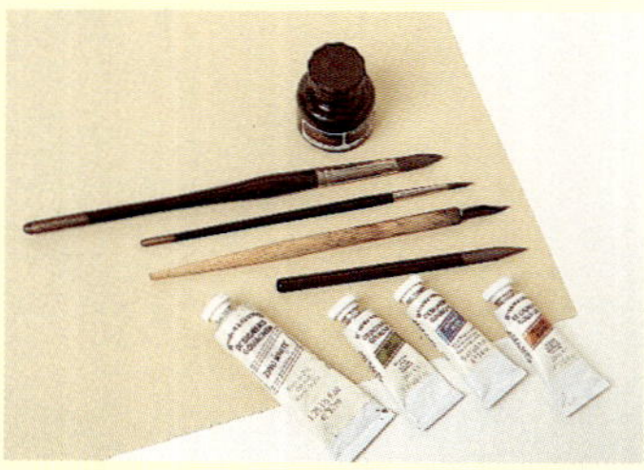

- One sheet of 15 x 22 in light-beige, 160 gsm Ingres paper
- Indian ink
- Gouache in the following colours: sap green, pthalo blue, yellow ochre and titanium white
- One pen with a medium nib
- Two sable watercolour brushes, one no 12 and one no 4

# The Drawing

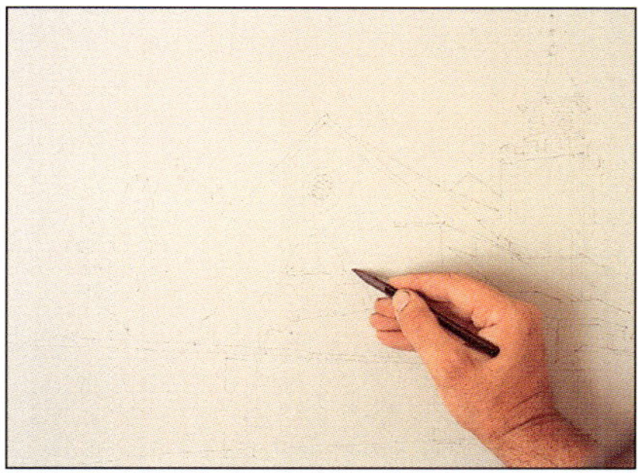

1 Using a soft pencil carefully sketch in and position the church on your sheet of paper. It is important to make certain that the angle of the building and the perspective look correct at this early stage, as this will help you with your drawing later on.

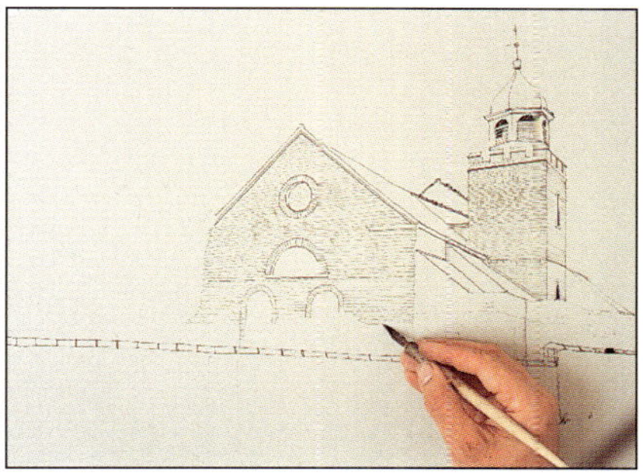

2 Dilute some black Indian ink and, working over the pencil drawing with the pen, carefully line in the shape of the louvered cupola, the tower and the main body of the church. Use neat black ink to darken and define the end of the tiled roofs and the louvres on the cupola. Darken the tower windows and draw in the line of the wall and its top row of stones. Use dilute ink to draw the brickwork and window surrounds of the church; add texture to the brickwork by wetting a finger with ink and using it to print across the walls.

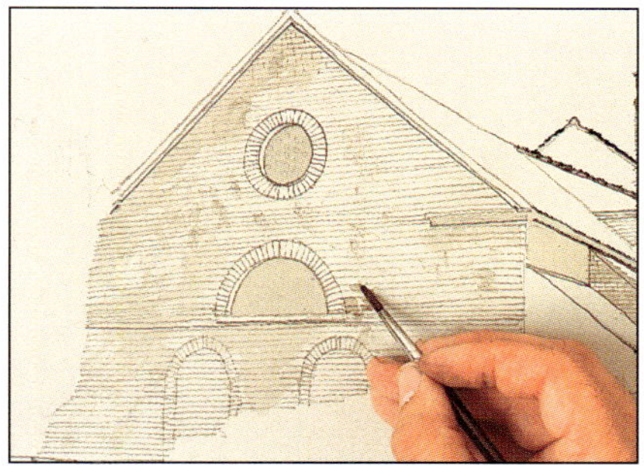

3 Take the smaller brush and, using the dilute ink, block in the dark areas of the windows. Now begin to add detail to some of the brickwork.

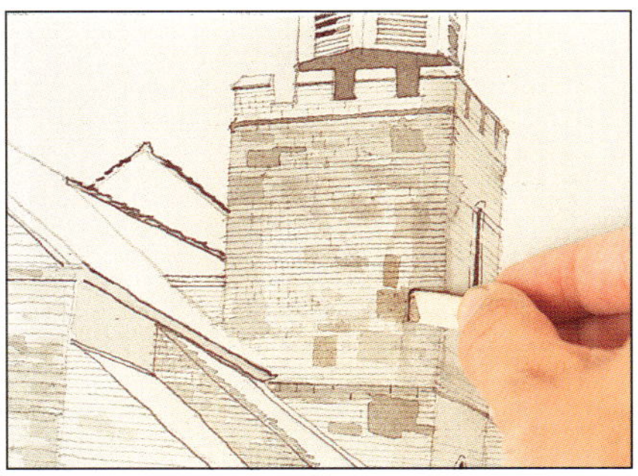

4 A different quality can be added by cutting a small piece of card, dipping the end in ink and using it to make brick and stone-shaped marks across the church walls.

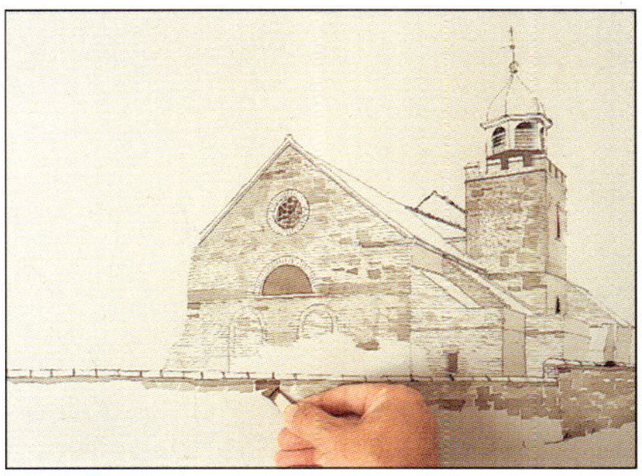

5 Use the same technique to indicate the brickwork along the wall in front of the church; varying the strength of the diluted ink gives a variety of tone. Indicate the dark areas on the round window by dabbing ink on with a small brush. Using the brush, draw in the tiled roof.

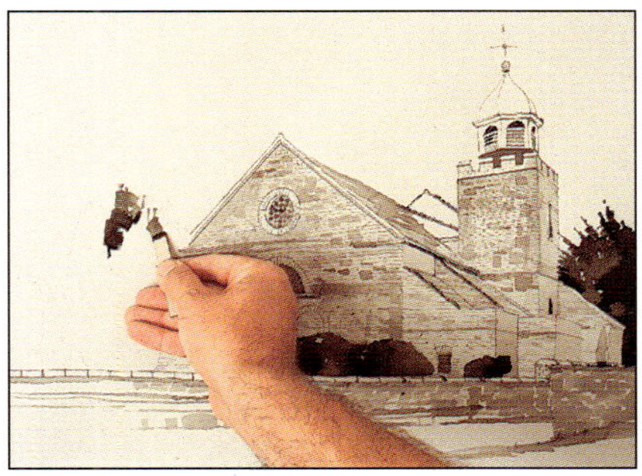

6 Using a dark green mix of ink, gouache and water, apply the same technique to draw in the ancient yews and bushes in the churchyard, and the line of grass at the base of the wall. As the piece of cardboard you are working with becomes softened by the ink you will need to recut the end, or replace it with a new piece of card.

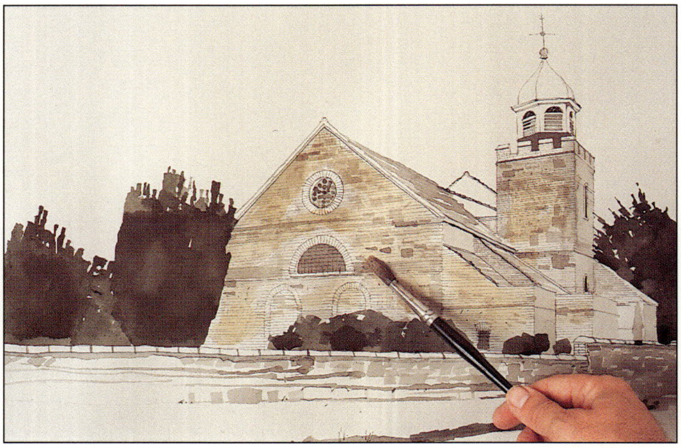

7 A light wash of ochre gouache is brushed over the stonework wall of the building with the larger sable brush. This serves to set the building apart from the stone wall in the foreground.

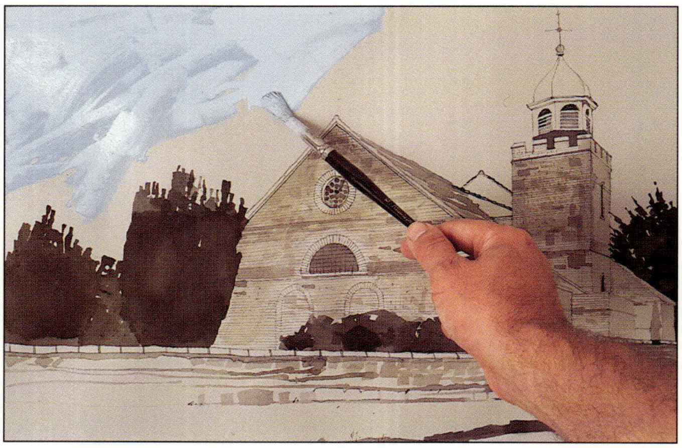

8 The same brush is then used to wash on a layer of light blue, mixed from white and pthalo blue gouache. Work loosely up to the trees and the church. Allow this to dry before brushing over the white. Do not be too concerned about bringing the sky right up to the building and the trees.

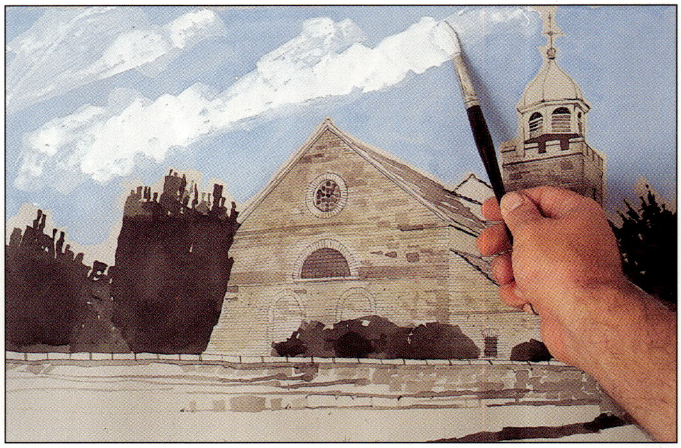

9 Clouds are painted using neat white gouache. As the gouache dries the intensity of the white diminishes; a second coat will help to lighten them.

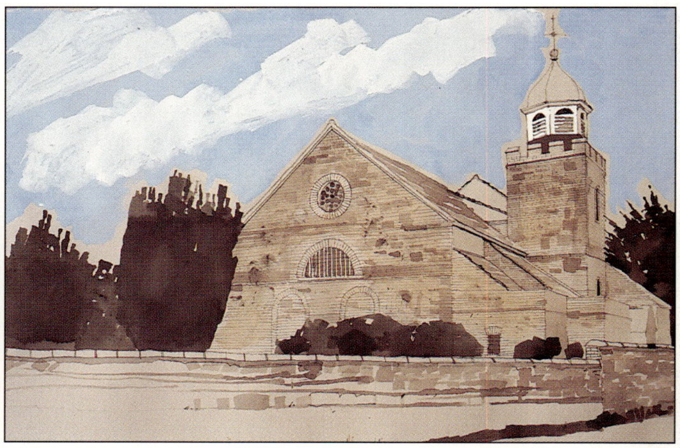

10 The painting is completed by lightening the cupola with white and, with the smaller brush, indicating the grill across the window. Finally, a few dark thumb and finger prints liven up the brickwork on the church.

# Alternative Approaches

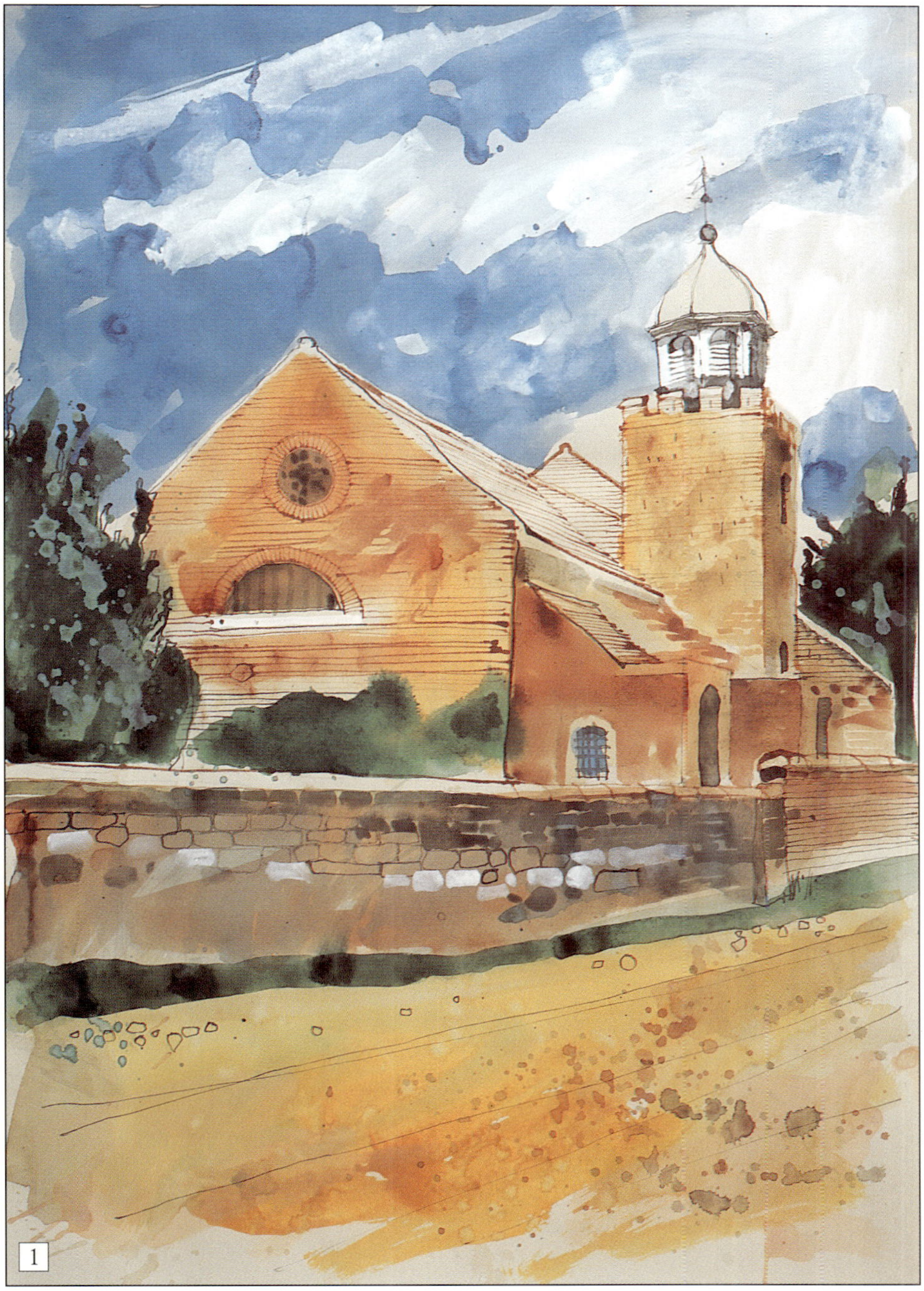

1

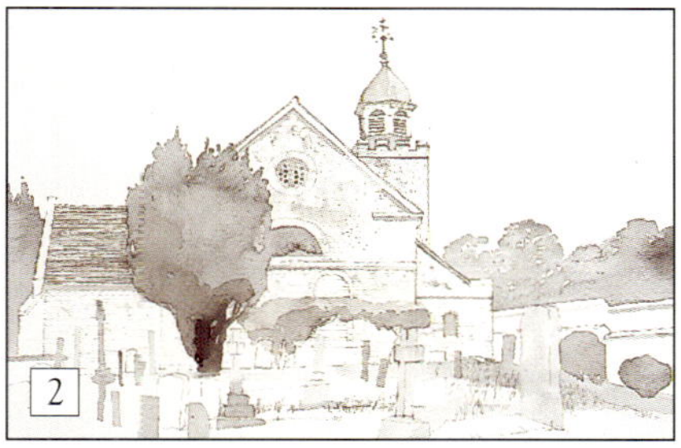

2

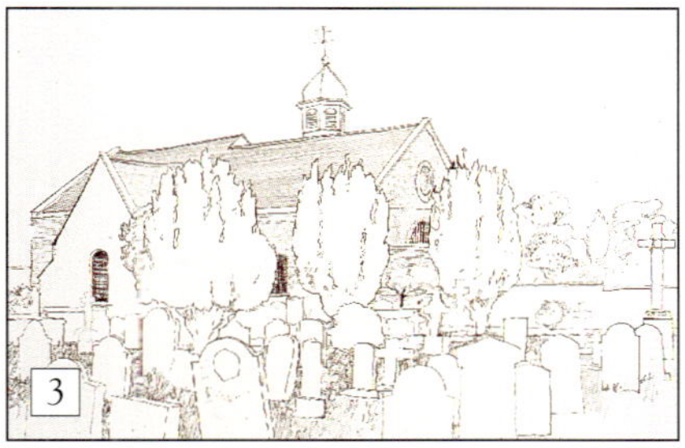

3

1 Bright acrylic inks give colour to this lively and decorative rendition, drawn from a similar view.

2 By drawing the church end-on the linear perspective is almost non-existent, except for very top of the cupola and the stone wall on the extreme right. Distance is shown by the dark yew in the foreground, which visually pushes forward, and the lighter row of trees in the background receding. This is achieved by painting the trees in the distance with a more dilute mix of ink and water.

3 In this drawing no attempt has been made to fill in any areas of tone. The dark, almost black yew trees are shown as white shapes, the clumps of foliage in outline only.

# INDEX